THE BOOK OF

LIGHT SAUCES
& SALAD DRESSINGS

THE BOOK OF

LIGHT SAUCES
& SALAD DRESSINGS

ANNE SHEASBY

Photographed by
STEVE BAXTER

PUBLISHED BY
SALAMANDER BOOKS LIMITED
LONDON

Published by Salamander Books Limited
8 Blenheim court, Brewery Road, London N/ 9NT, United Kingdom

9 8 7 6 5 4 3

ISBN 1-84065-138-5

All correspondence concerning the content of this book
should be addressed to Salamander Books Ltd.

Managing Editor: Felicity Jackson
Art Director: Roger Daniels
Photographer: Steve Baxter, assisted by Karen Chang
Home Economist: Carole Handslip, assisted by Susana Handslip
Typeset by: Pearl Graphics, Hemel Hempstead
Colour separation by: Scantrans Pte. Ltd, Singapore
Printed and bound in Spain by Bookprint, S.L.

ACKNOWLEDGEMENTS

The publishers would like to thank the following for their help:
Meyer (UK) Ltd., for supplying the saucepans.

Notes:
All spoon measurements are level.
1 teaspoon = 5 ml spoon.
1 tablespoon = 15 ml spoon.

CONTENTS

INTRODUCTION

A good sauce will provide the finishing touch to numerous dishes. A sauce enhances the flavour of food, both sweet and savoury, and can transform a dish into something special.

Many sauces are traditionally associated with certain foods, but sauces are also very versatile and can be served with a wide variety of dishes.

More unusual sauces can make a pleasant change and by choosing different ingredients, you can create appetising sauces to suit all kinds of foods and tastes.

Sauces are simple to make once the basic techniques have been mastered and they don't need to be high in calories or fat to make them appealing and delicious. By replacing some of the more traditional ingredients with lower calorie / lower fat alternatives, you can create light, healthy sauces, full of delicious flavours, colours and textures. You will be reducing your calorie and fat intakes, without even noticing the difference.

In this book, you will discover tasty light sauces, both sweet and savoury, plus a delicious selection of light salad dressings. Recipes include traditional sauces as well as more unusual light sauces and each recipe is illustrated in full colour with step-by-step instructions, showing you just what to expect.

Try some of these delicious light sauces and add that special finishing touch to your own dishes.

INGREDIENTS FOR LIGHT SAUCES

Nowadays, healthy eating is a very important part of our everyday lives and following basic, good, healthy eating patterns is essential for our general well-being.

Sauces are often thought of as the delicious, creamy, rich accompaniment to numerous dishes. Traditionally, many sauces are relatively high in calories and fat, but light sauces just as delicious and appetising can be made by making a few simple changes to the ingredients in the recipe, resulting in lower calorie/lower fat light sauces.

By reducing the amount of fat, sugar and salt you eat and increasing the amount of fibre in your diet, you will be making small changes in your eating habits, whilst taking positive steps towards eating a healthier diet.

The recipes use a whole range of different ingredients, all of which are widely and readily available.

LOW FAT

Low fat spread, skimmed or semi-skimmed milk, reduced fat creams and lower fat cheeses, have been used in place of some of the higher calorie and higher fat traditional ingredients, often used in sauce-making.

Low fat plain yogurt is a tasty, healthy alternative to milk or cream in some of the light sauces.

In place of butter or margarine, which contain very high fat contents, some of the recipes use low fat spread as an alternative. Low fat spread contains half the fat of butter or margarine and is suitable for melting. Low fat spreads do vary and you may need to experiment to see which one you like best. Very low fat spread is not suitable for sauces.

Oil has been used in some of the recipes, but only the polyunsaturated varieties such as sunflower oil, sesame oil and olive oil. Oils are high in

calories and fat and should be used sparingly. It is possible to reduce the amount of oil that would traditionally be used in many sauces and dressings without affecting the flavour or texture of the light sauce, as well as keeping it lower in calories and fat.

FRUIT AND VEGETABLES
Fruit and vegetable purées make an excellent low calorie/low fat basis for many light sauces and they add delightful flavours, colours and textures to many dishes, as well as increasing the dietary fibre content of the meal.

Fresh fruits have been used in the recipes as much as possible, as they are full of natural sugar and flavour.

When canned fruit has been used in recipes, use canned fruit in fruit juice rather than in syrup.

Fresh herbs and spices add delicious flavours and aromas to many of the

light sauces, without adding many calories or fat.

SALAD DRESSINGS
The chapter on light salad dressings incorporates a wide choice of delicious dressings for all kinds of salads from simple leaf salads to meat, fish and pasta salads, all with far fewer calories than ordinary salad dressings.

SERVING SUGGESTIONS
Serving suggestions appear at the end of each recipe, but use your imagination – many of the light sauces are very versatile and can be served with a wide variety of dishes. Many of the recipes are suitable for vegetarians too.

Each recipe shows the total amount of light sauce the recipe makes, as well as calorie and fat contents of each recipe per tablespoon of the cooked light sauce.

BASIC WHITE SAUCE

25 g (1 oz/6 teaspoons) low fat spread
25 g (1 oz/¼ cup) plain flour
300 ml (10 fl oz/1 ¼ cups) semi-skimmed milk
salt and pepper

In a saucepan, melt low fat spread over a low heat. Stir in flour and cook for 1 minute, stirring.

Remove pan from heat and gradually stir or whisk in the milk. Bring slowly to the boil, stirring or whisking, and continue to cook until the mixture thickens.

Simmer gently for 3 minutes. Remove pan from heat and season with salt and pepper. Serve with meat, poultry, fish or vegetables.

Makes 300 ml (10 fl oz/1 ¼ cups/20 tbsp).

Calories per tablespoon: 16 Kcals/67 Kj
Fat per tablespoon: 0.7 g

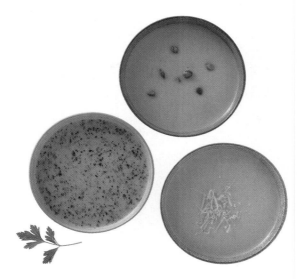

— WHITE SAUCE VARIATIONS —

CHEESE SAUCE
Follow the recipe for Basic White Sauce. Before seasoning with salt and pepper, stir in 55 g (2 oz/½ cup) grated reduced-fat Cheddar cheese and 1 teaspoon prepared mustard. Serve with fish, poultry, ham, vegetables or egg dishes.

Calories per tablespoon: 23 Kcals/98 Kj
Fat per tablespoon: 1.2 g

PARSLEY SAUCE
Follow the recipe for Basic White Sauce. After seasoning with salt and pepper, stir in 2 tablespoons finely chopped fresh parsley. Serve with fish, ham or bacon.

Calories per tablespoon: 16 Kcals/67 Kj
Fat per tablespoon: 0.7 g

CAPER SAUCE
Follow the recipe for Basic White Sauce. Before seasoning with salt and pepper, stir in 2 tablespoons capers and 2 teaspoons vinegar from the jar of capers. Reheat gently before serving. Serve with lamb.

Calories per tablespoon: 16 Kcals/67 Kj
Fat per tablespoon: 0.7 g

ESPAGNOLE SAUCE

1 rasher lean back bacon
25 g (1 oz/6 teaspoons) low fat spread
1 small onion or shallot
1 small carrot
55 g (2 oz) mushrooms
9 teaspoons plain flour
550 ml (20 fl oz/2½ cups) beef stock
1 bouquet garni
4 black peppercorns
1 bay leaf
2 tablespoons tomato purée (paste)
salt and pepper

Trim the rind and fat from the bacon and chop the bacon finely.

In a saucepan, melt low fat spread over a low heat. Add bacon and cook for 2 minutes, stirring. Chop onion or shallot, carrot and mushrooms finely. Add vegetables to the bacon and cook for 5-10 minutes until lightly browned, stirring occasionally. Stir in flour and cook until lightly browned, stirring continuously. Remove pan from heat and gradually stir in stock. Add all the remaining ingredients and bring slowly to the boil, stirring, until the mixture thickens. Cover and simmer gently for 1 hour, stirring occasionally.

Strain the sauce, remove bouquet garni and rub the pulp through a sieve. Discard the remaining pulp and return sauce to a saucepan. Reheat gently and adjust the seasoning before serving. Serve with red meats or game.

Makes 425 ml (15 fl oz/1¾ cups/28 tbsp).

Calories per tablespoon: 12 Kcals/50 Kj
Fat per tablespoon: 0.5 g

BÉCHAMEL SAUCE

1 small onion or shallot
1 small carrot
½ stick celery
1 bay leaf
6 black peppercorns
several stalks parsley
300 ml (10 fl oz/1¼ cups) semi-skimmed milk
25 g (1 oz/6 teaspoons) low fat spread
25 g (1 oz/¼ cup) plain flour
salt and pepper

Slice the onion or shallot and carrot. Chop the celery roughly. Put vegetables and flavourings in a saucepan with milk and bring slowly to the boil.

Remove pan from heat, cover and set aside to infuse for 30 minutes. Strain into a jug, reserving the milk. In a saucepan, melt low fat spread over a low heat. Stir in flour and cook for 1 minute, stirring.

Remove pan from heat and gradually stir or whisk in flavoured milk. Bring slowly to the boil, stirring or whisking, and continue to cook until the mixture thickens. Simmer gently for 3 minutes. Remove pan from heat and season with salt and pepper. Serve with poultry, fish, vegetables or egg dishes.

Makes 300 ml (10 fl oz/1¼ cups/20 tbsp).

Calories per tablespoon: 18 Kcals/75 Kj
Fat per tablespoon: 0.8 g

TRADITIONAL GRAVY

1 small onion
25 g (1 oz/6 teaspoons) low fat spread
25 g (1 oz/¼ cup) plain flour
300 ml (10 fl oz/1¼ cups) beef stock
1 tablespoon tomato purée (paste)
1 teaspoon sugar
1 teaspoon yeast extract
1 teaspoon dried mixed herbs
salt and pepper

Chop onion finely. In a saucepan, melt low fat spread over a low heat. Add onion and cook for 5 minutes until soft, stirring.

Stir in flour and cook gently for 1 minute, stirring. Remove pan from heat and gradually stir in stock. Add the remaining ingredients and bring slowly to the boil, stirring. Continue to cook until the mixture thickens, then simmer gently for 3 minutes.

Adjust the seasoning and serve with grilled or roast red meats, such as beef, lamb or pork.

Makes 425 ml (15 fl oz/1¾ cups/28 tbsp).

Calories per tablespoon: 9 Kcals/36 Kj
Fat per tablespoon: 0.4 g

Variation: Use chicken stock instead of beef stock, if serving the gravy with poultry.

ONION SAUCE

1 onion
25 g (1 oz/6 teaspoons) low fat spread
25 g (1 oz/¼ cup) plain flour
450 ml (16 fl oz/2 cups) semi-skimmed milk
salt and pepper

Chop onion finely. In a saucepan, melt low fat spread over a low heat. Add onion and cook for 8-10 minutes, until soft, stirring occasionally.

Stir in flour and cook for 1 minute, stirring. Remove pan from heat and gradually stir in milk. Bring slowly to the boil, stirring, and continue to cook until the mixture thickens.

Simmer gently for 3 minutes. Remove pan from heat and season with salt and pepper. Serve with lamb or egg dishes.

Makes 550 ml (20 fl oz/2½ cups/36 tbsp).

Calories per tablespoon: 12 Kcals/50 Kj
Fat per tablespoon: 0.5 g

PIQUANT SAUCE

1 small onion
1 small carrot
55 g (2 oz) mushrooms
25 g (1 oz/6 teaspoons) low fat spread
25 g (1 oz/¼ cup) plain flour
550 ml (20 fl oz/2½ cups) vegetable stock
1 bay leaf
salt and pepper
1 tablespoon capers
25 g (1 oz) gherkins
1 tablespoon chopped fresh parsley

Chop the onion, carrot and mushrooms finely. In a saucepan, melt low fat spread over a low heat.

Add onion, carrot and mushrooms and cook for 8-10 minutes until soft, stirring occasionally. Stir in flour and cook for 1 minute, stirring. Remove pan from heat and gradually stir in stock. Bring slowly to the boil, stirring, and continue to cook until the mixture thickens. Add bay leaf and salt and pepper, cover and simmer gently for 30 minutes, stirring occasionally. Chop the capers and gherkins finely. Remove the bay leaf from the sauce and discard.

Stir the chopped capers, gherkins and parsley into the sauce. Reheat gently, adjust the seasoning and serve with fish or red meats.

Makes 750 ml (26 fl oz/3½ cups/50 tbsp).

Calories per tablespoon: 5 Kcals/21 Kj
Fat per tablespoon: 0.2 g

Variation: Try using your own mixture of vegetables in the recipe, such as tomatoes, spring onions and celery.

MUSTARD SAUCE

25 g (1 oz/6 teaspoons) low fat spread
25 g (1 oz/¼ cup) plain flour
300 ml (10 fl oz/1¼ cups) semi-skimmed milk
6 teaspoons wholegrain mustard
salt and pepper

In a saucepan, melt low fat spread over a low heat. Stir in flour and cook for 1 minute, stirring.

Remove pan from heat and gradually stir or whisk in the milk. Bring slowly to the boil, stirring or whisking, and continue to cook until mixture thickens. Simmer gently for 3 minutes.

Stir in mustard and season with salt and pepper. Reheat gently before serving. Serve with oily fish, ham, bacon, vegetables or cheese dishes.

Makes 350 ml (12 fl oz/1½ cups/23 tbsp).

Calories per tablespoon: 15 Kcals/64 Kj
Fat per tablespoon: 0.8 g

TARRAGON SAUCE

25 g (1 oz/6 teaspoons) low fat spread
25 g (1 oz/¼ cup) plain flour
300 ml (10 fl oz/1¼ cups) chicken stock
150 ml (5 fl oz/⅔ cup) semi-skimmed milk
2 tablespoons tarragon vinegar
few sprigs tarragon
2 teaspoons smooth mustard
55 g (2 oz/½ cup) reduced-fat Cheddar cheese
salt and pepper

In a saucepan, melt low fat spread over a low heat. Stir in flour and cook for 1 minute, stirring. Remove pan from heat and gradually stir or whisk in stock, milk and vinegar.

Bring slowly to the boil, stirring or whisking, and continue to cook until the mixture thickens. Simmer gently for 3 minutes. Chop the tarragon finely.

Stir the tarragon into the sauce with the mustard, cheese and salt and pepper and reheat gently, but do not allow the mixture to boil. Serve with chicken or turkey.

Makes 550 ml (20 fl oz/2½ cups/36 tbsp).

Calories per tablespoon: 11 Kcals/47 Kj
Fat per tablespoon: 0.6 g

PAPRIKA SAUCE

1 small onion
25 g (1 oz/6 teaspoons) low fat spread
25 g (1 oz/¼ cup) plain flour
1 teaspoon paprika
200 ml (7 fl oz/¾ cup) semi-skimmed milk
70 ml (2½ fl oz/⅓ cup) dry sherry
salt and pepper

Chop onion finely. In a saucepan, melt low fat spread over a low heat. Add onion and cook for 5 minutes, stirring.

Whisk in flour and paprika and cook for 1 minute, stirring. Remove pan from heat and gradually whisk in milk and sherry.

Bring slowly to the boil, whisking, and continue to cook gently for 3 minutes. Remove pan from heat and season with salt and pepper. Serve with vegetables such as cauliflower or marrow.

Makes 325 ml (11 fl oz/1⅓ cups/21 tbsp).

Calories per tablespoon: 19 Kcals/81 Kj
Fat per tablespoon: 0.7 g

──LEMON & CHERVIL SAUCE──

25 g (1 oz/6 teaspoons) low fat spread
9 teaspoons plain flour
150 ml (5 fl oz/²⁄₃ cup) chicken stock
150 ml (5 fl oz/²⁄₃ cup) semi-skimmed milk
few sprigs chervil
finely grated rind and juice of 1 lemon
salt and pepper

In a saucepan, melt low fat spread over a low heat. Stir in flour and cook for 1 minute, stirring. Remove pan from heat and gradually stir or whisk in stock and milk.

Bring slowly to the boil, stirring or whisking, and continue to cook until the mixture thickens. Simmer gently for 3 minutes. Chop chervil finely.

Stir chervil into sauce with lemon rind and lemon juice and season with salt and pepper. Reheat the sauce gently before serving. Serve with fish such as cod, haddock, plaice or salmon.

Makes 300 ml (10 fl oz/1¼ cups/20 tbsp).

Calories per tablespoon: 17 Kcals/70 Kj
Fat per serving: 0.7 g

BORDELAISE SAUCE

1 rasher lean back bacon
25 g (1 oz/6 teaspoons) low fat spread
2 shallots
1 carrot
55 g (2 oz) mushrooms
9 teaspoons plain flour
300 ml (10 fl oz/1¼ cups) beef stock
300 ml (10 fl oz/1¼ cups) red wine
1 bouquet garni
salt and pepper

Trim rind and fat from the bacon and chop the bacon finely. In a saucepan, melt low fat spread over a low heat. Add bacon and cook for 2 minutes, stirring.

Chop shallots, carrot and mushrooms finely. Add to bacon and cook for 5-10 minutes until lightly browned, stirring occasionally. Add flour and cook until lightly browned, stirring continuously. Remove pan from heat and gradually stir in stock and wine.

Bring slowly to the boil, stirring, and continue to cook until the mixture thickens. Add the bouquet garni and season with salt and pepper. Cover and simmer gently for 1 hour, stirring occasionally. Strain the sauce, adjust the seasoning and serve with red meats or game.

Makes 400 ml (14 fl oz/1¾ cups/26 tbsp).

Calories per tablespoon: 21 Kcals/87 Kj
Fat per tablespoon: 0.5 g

MUSHROOM SAUCE

1 small onion
1 small carrot
½ stick celery
1 bay leaf
6 black peppercorns
450 ml (16 fl oz/2 cups) semi-skimmed milk
175 g (6 oz) button mushrooms
55 g (2 oz/¼ cup) low fat spread
55 g (2 oz/½ cup) plain flour
salt and pepper

Slice the onion and carrot. Chop celery roughly. Put vegetables and flavourings in a saucepan with the milk and slowly bring to the boil.

Remove pan from heat, cover and set aside to infuse for 30 minutes. Strain into a jug, reserving the milk. Slice mushrooms thinly. In a saucepan, melt low fat spread over a low heat. Add mushrooms and cook for 5 minutes until soft, stirring occasionally. Stir in flour and cook for 1 minute, stirring. Remove pan from heat and gradually stir in the flavoured milk.

Bring slowly to the boil, stirring, and continue to cook until the mixture thickens. Simmer gently for 3 minutes. Remove pan from heat and season with salt and pepper. Serve with fish or vegetables such as broccoli or potatoes.

Makes 550 ml (20 fl oz/2½ cups/36 tbsp).

Calories per tablespoon: 18 Kcals/75 Kj
Fat per tablespoon: 0.9 g

RED WINE SAUCE

1 small onion
1 clove garlic
25 g (1 oz/6 teaspoons) low fat spread
25 g (1 oz/¼ cup) plain flour
250 ml (9 fl oz/1 cup) beef stock
200 ml (7 fl oz/¾ cup) red wine
2 teaspoons chopped fresh thyme
1 tablespoon lemon juice
salt and pepper

Grate onion finely and crush garlic. In a saucepan, melt low fat spread over a low heat. Add onion and garlic and cook for 5 minutes, stirring occasionally.

Stir in flour and cook for 1 minute, stirring. Remove pan from heat and gradually stir in stock and wine. Bring slowly to the boil, stirring, and continue to cook until the mixture thickens. Simmer gently for 3 minutes.

Stir the chopped thyme into the sauce with the lemon juice and season with salt and pepper. Reheat the sauce gently before serving. Serve with beef.

Makes 500 ml (18 fl oz/2¼ cups/33 tbsp).

Calories per tablespoon: 10 Kcals/41 Kj
Fat per tablespoon: 0.3 g

Variation: Use medium white wine in place of the red wine for a white wine sauce and serve it with poultry or fish.

CELERY SAUCE

1 small onion
225 g (8 oz) celery
25 g (1 oz/6 teaspoons) low fat spread
25 g (1 oz/¼ cup) plain flour
150 ml (5 fl oz/⅔ cup) semi-skimmed milk
150 ml (5 fl oz/⅔ cup) vegetable stock
salt and pepper

Chop onion and celery finely. In a saucepan, melt low fat spread over a low heat.

Add onion and celery to pan and cook for 8-10 minutes until soft, stirring occasionally. Stir in flour and cook for 1 minute, stirring. Remove pan from heat and gradually stir in milk and stock. Bring slowly to the boil, stirring, and continue to cook until the mixture thickens.

Simmer gently for 3 minutes. Remove pan from heat and season with salt and pepper. Serve with roast chicken or turkey.

Makes 550 ml (20 fl oz/2½ cups/36 tbsp).

Calories per tablespoon: 8 Kcals/34 Kj
Fat per tablespoon: 0.4 g

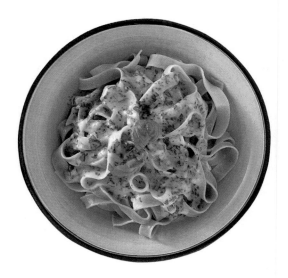

FRESH BASIL SAUCE

1 small onion or shallot
1 clove garlic
15 g (½ oz/3 teaspoons) low fat spread
15 g (½ oz/6 teaspoons) plain flour
300 ml (10 fl oz/1 ¼ cups) semi-skimmed milk
25 g (1 oz) fresh Parmesan cheese
2 tablespoons chopped fresh basil
salt and pepper

Finely chop onion or shallot and crush garlic. In a saucepan, melt low fat spread over a low heat. Add onion or shallot and garlic and cook for 5 minutes, stirring.

Stir in flour and cook for 1 minute, stirring. Remove pan from heat and gradually whisk in the milk. Bring slowly to the boil, whisking, and continue to cook until the mixture thickens. Simmer gently for 3 minutes. Grate the Parmesan cheese finely.

Whisk basil and Parmesan into sauce and season with salt and pepper. Reheat gently before serving. Serve with chicken, fish or pasta.

Makes 350 ml (12 fl oz/1 ½ cups/23 tbsp).

Calories per tablespoon: 16 Kcals/67 Kj
Fat per tablespoon: 0.8 g

──QUICK TOMATO SAUCE──

1 clove garlic
1 tablespoon chopped mixed fresh herbs, such as
    parsley, thyme, rosemary and chives
400 g (14 oz) can chopped tomatoes
150 ml (5 fl oz/⅔ cup) dry white wine
1 tablespoon tomato purée (paste)
salt and pepper
3 teaspoons cornflour

Crush garlic. Put garlic, herbs, tomatoes, wine, tomato purée (paste) and salt and pepper in a saucepan and mix well.

Bring slowly to the boil, cover and simmer gently for 20 minutes, stirring occasionally. In a small bowl, blend the cornflour with 1 tablespoon water.

Stir cornflour mixture into tomato sauce, mixing well and bring the sauce back to the boil, stirring. Simmer gently for 3 minutes. Adjust the seasoning before serving. Serve with fish, meat or poultry.

Makes 550 ml (20 fl oz/2½ cups/36 tbsp).

Calories per tablespoon: 6 Kcals/25 Kj
Fat per tablespoon: 0.02 g

WATERCRESS SAUCE

1 small onion
1 clove garlic
2 bunches watercress
25 g (1 oz/6 teaspoons) low fat spread
25 g (1 oz/¼ cup) plain flour
300 ml (10 fl oz/1¼ cups) semi-skimmed milk
150 ml (5 fl oz/⅔ cup) chicken stock
salt and pepper

Chop onion finely. Crush garlic and chop watercress finely. In a saucepan, melt low fat spread over a low heat. Add onion, garlic and watercress and cook for 5 minutes until soft, stirring occasionally.

Stir in flour and cook for 1 minute, stirring. Remove pan from heat and gradually stir or whisk in milk and stock and season with salt and pepper. Bring slowly to the boil, stirring or whisking, and continue to cook until the mixture thickens. Cover and simmer gently for 5 minutes. Remove pan from heat and set aside to cool.

When cool, purée the sauce in a blender or food processor until smooth. Return the sauce to a saucepan, reheat gently and adjust the seasoning before serving. Serve with lamb, fish or savoury pies or quiches.

Makes 550 ml (20 fl oz/2½ cups/36 tbsp).

Calories per tablespoon: 8 Kcals/34 Kj
Fat per tablespoon: 0.4 g

—MUSHROOM & SAGE SAUCE—

2 shallots
350 g (12 oz) chestnut (brown cap) mushrooms
2 teaspoons olive oil
300 ml (10 fl oz/1¼ cups) vegetable stock
300 ml (10 fl oz/1¼ cups) semi-skimmed milk
2 tablespoons chopped fresh sage
1 bay leaf
salt and pepper
3 teaspoons cornflour

Chop shallots and mushrooms finely. In a saucepan, heat oil for 1 minute. Add shallots and mushrooms and cook for 8-10 minutes until soft, stirring.

Stir in stock and milk. Add chopped sage to saucepan with bay leaf and season with salt and pepper, mixing well. Bring slowly to the boil, cover and simmer gently for 30 minutes, stirring occasionally. Remove and discard bay leaf.

In a small bowl, blend cornflour with 2 table-spoons cold water. Stir the cornflour mixture into the sauce and bring slowly back to the boil, stirring continuously. Simmer gently for 3 minutes and adjust the seasoning before serving. Serve with chicken, fish or veal.

Makes 900 ml (32 fl oz/4 cups/60 tbsp).

Calories per tablespoon: 6 Kcals/25 Kj
Fat per tablespoon: 0.3 g

—— SWEET RED PEPPER SAUCE ——

2 red peppers (capsicums) (see Note)
6 spring onions
2 cloves garlic
1 sprig rosemary
300 ml (10 fl oz/1¼ cups) vegetable stock
salt and pepper

Seed peppers (capsicums) and chop finely. Trim and slice spring onions thinly. Crush garlic and chop rosemary finely. Put peppers (capsicums), spring onions, garlic, rosemary, stock and salt and pepper in a saucepan.

Bring mixture slowly to the boil, cover and simmer for 20 minutes until the vegetables are soft, stirring occasionally. Remove pan from heat and set aside to cool. Once cool, purée the sauce in a blender or food processor until smooth. Return the sauce to a saucepan.

Reheat gently and adjust the seasoning before serving. Serve hot or cold with vegetable dishes such as a vegetable terrine.

Makes 500 ml (18 fl oz/2¼ cups/33 tbsp).

Calories per tablespoon: 4 Kcals/17 Kj
Fat per tablespoon: 0.06 g

Note: The peppers (capsicums) may be peeled if wished. Place under a hot grill and cook for 8-10 minutes, turning frequently. Rub skins off under cold water.

-CARROT & CORIANDER SAUCE-

1 onion
450 g (1 lb) carrots
2 teaspoons sunflower oil
2 tablespoons chopped fresh coriander
300 ml (10 fl oz/1¼ cups) vegetable stock
salt and pepper

Chop onion finely and grate carrots coarsely. In a saucepan, heat oil for 1 minute. Add the onion and carrots and cook for 8 minutes, stirring.

Add the chopped coriander to carrots with stock and salt and pepper. Bring slowly to the boil, cover and simmer gently for 15-20 minutes, stirring occasionally. Remove pan from heat and set aside to cool.

Once cool, purée the sauce in a blender or food processor until smooth. Return the sauce to a saucepan. Reheat gently and adjust the seasoning before serving. Serve with poultry or game.

Makes 750 ml (26 fl oz/3½ cups/50 tbsp).

Calories per tablespoon: 6 Kcals/25 Kj
Fat per tablespoon: 0.2 g

Variation: Try using different herbs in place of coriander, such as parsley, thyme, chives.

HORSERADISH SAUCE

4 tablespoons grated fresh horseradish
1 teaspoon caster sugar
2 teaspoons smooth mustard
salt and pepper
2 tablespoons malt vinegar
9 teaspoons low fat plain yogurt

Place the grated horseradish in a bowl. Add sugar, mustard and salt and pepper and mix well.

Stir in vinegar, then gently stir in the yogurt, mixing well. Leave the horseradish sauce in a cool place for 30 minutes before serving, to allow the flavours to develop.

Serve with beef or oily fish.

Makes 150 ml (5 fl oz/²/₃ cup/10 tbsp).

Calories per tablespoon: 10 Kcals/41 Kj
Fat per tablespoon: 0.1 g

Variation: Use reduced fat single (light) cream in place of the plain yogurt, but remember this will increase the calorie and fat contents of the sauce.

Calories per tablespoon: 13 Kcals/53 Kj
Fat per tablespoon: 0.5 g

CHILLI SAUCE

4 spring onions
1 red chilli
1 clove garlic
3 teaspoons peanut oil
400 g (14 oz) can chopped tomatoes
1 tablespoon lemon juice
3 teaspoons soft brown sugar
salt and pepper
2 teaspoons cornflour

Trim and chop spring onions finely. Seed and chop chilli finely and crush garlic.

In a saucepan, heat oil for 1 minute. Add onions, chilli and garlic and cook for 5 minutes, stirring. Add tomatoes, lemon juice, sugar and salt and pepper. Bring slowly to the boil, cover and simmer gently for 10 minutes, stirring occasionally.

In a small bowl, blend cornflour with 1 tablespoon water. Stir cornflour mixture into the chilli sauce and bring the sauce to the boil, stirring continuously. Simmer gently for 3 minutes and adjust the seasoning before serving. Serve with fish, seafood or stuffed vegetables.

Makes 450 ml (16 fl oz/2 cups/30 tbsp).

Calories per tablespoon: 11 Kcals/47 Kj
Fat per tablespoon: 0.5 g

── SPINACH & GARLIC SAUCE ──

300 g (10 oz) fresh spinach
150 ml (5 fl oz/²⁄₃ cup) vegetable stock
4 cloves garlic
1 tablespoon chopped mixed fresh herbs, such as
    parsley, thyme, rosemary and chives
1 teaspoon ground cumin
salt and pepper

Chop spinach roughly and place in a saucepan with stock. Cover the saucepan, bring the mixture to the boil and boil for 5 minutes until spinach is soft. Crush garlic cloves.

Stir garlic, herbs, cumin and salt and pepper into the spinach mixture, mixing well. Bring slowly to the boil, cover and simmer gently for 10 minutes, stirring occasionally. Remove the pan from the heat and set aside to cool.

Once cool, purée the sauce in a blender or food processor until smooth. Return the sauce to a saucepan. Reheat gently and adjust the seasoning before serving. Serve with beef, fish or egg dishes.

Makes 500 ml (18 fl oz/2¼ cups/33 tbsp).

Calories per tablespoon: 3 Kcals/12 Kj
Fat per tablespoon: 0.1 g

CURRY SAUCE

1 onion
1 clove garlic
2 teaspoons sunflower oil
225 g (8 oz) potatoes
225 g (8 oz) can chopped tomatoes
300 ml (10 fl oz/1¼ cups) vegetable stock
3 teaspoons curry powder
1 teaspoon ground bay leaves
salt and pepper
55 g (2 oz/⅓ cup) sultanas

Chop onion finely and crush garlic. In a saucepan, heat oil for 1 minute. Add onion and garlic and cook for 5 minutes, stirring.

Peel and grate potatoes coarsely. Add potatoes, tomatoes, stock, curry powder, ground bay leaves and salt and pepper to the saucepan and mix well. Bring slowly to the boil, cover and simmer gently for 30 minutes, stirring occasionally. Remove pan from the heat and set aside to cool. Once cool, purée the sauce in a blender or food processor until smooth.

Return the sauce to a saucepan and add the sultanas. Reheat gently and adjust the seasoning before serving. Serve with vegetables or egg dishes.

Makes 800 ml (28 fl oz/3½ cups/53 tbsp).

Calories per tablespoon: 11 Kcals/47 Kj
Fat per tablespoon: 0.2 g

Variation: The sultanas can be added with the potatoes and tomatoes and puréed, if preferred.

──── PARSLEY & CHIVE SAUCE ────

25 g (1 oz/6 teaspoons) low fat spread
25 g (1 oz/¼ cup) plain flour
300 ml (10 fl oz/1¼ cups) semi-skimmed milk
2 tablespoons chopped fresh parsley
2 tablespoons chopped fresh chives
salt and pepper

In a saucepan, melt low fat spread over a low heat. Stir in flour and cook for 1 minute, stirring.

Remove pan from heat and gradually whisk in the milk. Bring slowly to the boil, whisking, and continue to cook until the mixture thickens.

Simmer gently for 3 minutes. Remove pan from heat and stir in herbs and salt and pepper. Serve with bacon, ham or fish.

Makes 350 ml (12 fl oz/1½ cups/23 tbsp).

Calories per tablespoon: 14 Kcals/59 Kj
Fat per tablespoon: 0.7 g

— SAGE & RED ONION SAUCE —

2 red onions
25 g (1 oz/6 teaspoons) low fat spread
25 g (1 oz/¼ cup) plain flour
150 ml (5 fl oz/⅔ cup) semi-skimmed milk
juice of 1 lime
2 tablespoons chopped fresh sage
salt and pepper

Chop onions finely. Put onions in a saucepan with 300 ml (10 fl oz/1¼ cups) water. Bring to the boil, cover and simmer gently for 10 minutes until the onions are soft. Strain onions, reserving 150 ml (5 fl oz/⅔ cup) of the cooking liquid.

In a saucepan, melt low fat spread over a low heat. Add onions and cook for 5 minutes, stirring. Stir in flour and cook for 1 minute, stirring. Remove pan from the heat and gradually stir in reserved stock, the milk and lime juice.

Bring slowly to the boil, stirring, and continue to cook until the mixture thickens. Simmer gently for 3 minutes. Remove pan from heat. Stir chopped sage into sauce. Season with salt and pepper, mixing well. Serve with poultry or game.

Makes 500 ml (18 fl oz/2¼ cups/33 tbsp).

Calories per tablespoon: 11 Kcals/47 Kj
Fat per tablespoon: 0.4 g

—BROCCOLI & CHEESE SAUCE—

225 g (8 oz) broccoli
3 teaspoons cornflour
150 ml (5 fl oz/⅔ cup) dry white wine
1 clove garlic
150 g (5 oz) low fat soft cheese
salt and pepper

Trim broccoli and cook in a saucepan of boiling water for 10 minutes until tender. Drain, reserving 2 tablespoons of the cooking liquid. Cool the broccoli, then purée with reserved liquid in a blender or food processor until smooth. Set the puréed broccoli aside.

In a saucepan, blend cornflour with wine. Crush garlic and add to the wine mixture. Bring slowly to the boil, stirring continuously, until the mixture thickens. Simmer gently for 3 minutes.

Remove pan from heat and stir in soft cheese, puréed broccoli and salt and pepper, mixing well. Reheat gently and adjust the seasoning before serving. Serve hot or cold with poultry, beef or fish.

Makes 550 ml (20 fl oz/2½ cups/36 tbsp).

Calories per tablespoon: 13 Kcals/55 Kj
Fat per tablespoon: 0.6 g

—SPICY COURGETTE SAUCE—

2 courgettes (zucchini)
1 green pepper (capsicum)
1 small onion
1 clove garlic
25 g (1 oz/6 teaspoons) low fat spread
1 teaspoon ground coriander
½ teaspoon ground cumin
½ teaspoon ground chilli powder
¼ teaspoon cayenne pepper
¼ teaspoon turmeric
150 ml (5 fl oz/⅔ cup) vegetable stock
salt and pepper

Trim the courgettes (zucchini) and grate them coarsely.

Seed and chop pepper (capsicum) finely. Chop onion finely and crush garlic. In a saucepan, melt low fat spread over a low heat. Add courgettes (zucchini), pepper (capsicum), onion and garlic and cook for 5 minutes, stirring.

Stir in spices, stock and salt and pepper and mix well. Bring slowly to the boil, cover and simmer for 25 minutes, stirring occasionally. Remove pan from heat and set aside to cool. Once cool, purée mixture in a blender or food processor until smooth. Return the sauce to a saucepan. Reheat gently and adjust the seasoning before serving. Serve with seafood, fish or meat.

Makes 500 ml (18 fl oz/2¼ cups/33 tbsp).

Calories per tablespoon: 8 Kcals/34 Kj
Fat per tablespoon: 0.4 g

– BEETROOT & ORANGE SAUCE –

1 small onion or shallot
2 sticks celery
2 teaspoons sunflower oil
450 g (1 lb) uncooked beetroot
300 ml (10 fl oz/1¼ cups) vegetable stock
1 bay leaf
finely grated rind and juice of 1 orange
1 tablespoon chopped fresh parsley
salt and pepper
150 ml (5 fl oz/⅔ cup) sour cream

Chop onion or shallot and celery finely. In a saucepan, heat oil for 1 minute. Add onion or shallot and celery and cook for 3 minutes, stirring.

Peel and dice beetroot. Add to saucepan and cook for 3 minutes, stirring. Stir in stock and bay leaf and mix well. Bring slowly to the boil, cover and simmer for 1-1½ hours until the beetroot is soft. Remove and discard the bay leaf. Stir the orange rind, orange juice and parsley into the sauce and mix well. Remove the pan from the heat and set aside to cool.

Once cool, purée the mixture in a blender or food processor until smooth. Return the sauce to a saucepan. Reheat gently and season with salt and pepper. Remove pan from heat and stir in cream just before serving. Serve hot or cold with turkey, veal or oily fish.

Makes 800 ml (28 fl oz/3½ cups/53 tbsp).

Calories per tablespoon: 11 Kcals/47 Kj
Fat per tablespoon: 0.8 g

SALSA

2 cloves garlic
1 red chilli
2 tablespoons chopped mixed fresh herbs, such as
    parsley, thyme, rosemary and chives
400 g (14 oz) can chopped tomatoes
juice of 1 lime
salt and pepper

Crush garlic and seed and finely chop the
chilli.

Place garlic, chilli, chopped herbs, tomatoes,
lime juice and salt and pepper in a saucepan
and mix well.

Bring slowly to the boil and simmer,
uncovered, for 10 minutes, stirring occasionally. The salsa may be served hot or cold.
Serve with Mexican foods such as filled
tortillas.

Makes 200 ml (7 fl oz/¾ cup/13 tbsp).

Calories per tablespoon: 8 Kcals/34 Kj
Fat per tablespoon: 0.07 g

──────MINTY APPLE SAUCE──────

1 small onion
450 g (1 lb) cooking apples
small bunch fresh mint
25 g (1 oz/5 teaspoons) caster sugar

Chop onion finely. Peel, core and slice apples. Put onion and apples in a saucepan with 2 tablespoons water.

Cover saucepan and heat mixture gently until the apples and onion are soft. Remove pan from heat and mash the apples and onion lightly.

Chop mint finely and add to saucepan with the sugar, mixing well. Reheat sauce gently until the sugar has dissolved. Serve hot or cold with lamb or pork.

Makes 400 ml (14 fl oz/1¾ cups/26 tbsp).

Calories per tablespoon: 11 Kcals/47 Kj
Fat per tablespoon: 0.03 g

——FRESH TOMATO SAUCE——

6 spring onions
1 carrot
1 stick celery
1 clove garlic
1 teaspoon olive oil
700 g (1½ lb) tomatoes
1 tablespoon chopped fresh mixed herbs, such as
   parsley, thyme, rosemary and chives
1 teaspoon ground bay leaves
1 teaspoon caster sugar
2 tablespoons tomato purée (paste) (optional)
salt and pepper

Chop spring onions, carrot and celery finely. Crush garlic.

In a saucepan, heat oil for 1 minute. Add onions, carrot, celery and garlic and cook for 5 minutes, stirring. Peel and chop tomatoes roughly and add to saucepan with remaining ingredients. Bring slowly to the boil, cover and simmer for 15 minutes, stirring occasionally. Remove pan from heat and set aside to cool. Once cool, purée the mixture in a blender or food processor until smooth. Strain the puréed sauce through a nylon sieve, discarding the pulp. Return sauce to a saucepan. Reheat gently and adjust the seasoning before serving.

Serve with Greek dishes such as stuffed vine leaves or meatballs.

Makes 500 ml (18 fl oz/2¼ cups/33 tbsp).

Calories per tablespoon: 8 Kcals/34 Kj
Fat per tablespoon: 0.2 g

Note: A simple way to peel tomatoes is to place them in boiling water for about 30 seconds, then plunge them into cold water. The skins should then peel off easily.

——DILL & CUCUMBER SAUCE——

½ cucumber
1 tablespoon chopped fresh dill
300 ml (10 fl oz/1¼ cups) low fat plain yogurt
1 teaspoon smooth mustard
salt and pepper

Chop cucumber finely and place in a bowl.
Add chopped dill to cucumber, mixing well.

Stir in plain yogurt and mustard and mix
well. Season with salt and pepper. Stand the
sauce in a cool place for 30 minutes before
serving, to allow the flavours to develop.

Serve with white fish, oily fish or shellfish.

Makes 500 ml (18 fl oz/2¼ cups/33 tbsp).

Calories per tablespoon: 6 Kcals/25 Kj
Fat per tablespoon: 0.1 g

Variation: Use 150 ml (5 fl oz/⅔ cup) low fat
plain yogurt and 150 ml (5 fl oz/⅔ cup)
reduced fat single (light) cream, in place of
the low fat plain yogurt.

Calories per tablespoon: 9 Kcals/36 Kj
Fat per tablespoon: 0.5 g

SPICY LENTIL SAUCE

1 onion
1 carrot
2 sticks celery
2 teaspoons olive oil
225 g (8 oz/1⅓ cups) green lentils
1 tablespoon chopped fresh parsley
1 teaspoon ground cumin
1 teaspoon ground coriander
1 teaspoon ground allspice
1 teaspoon cayenne pepper
salt and pepper
550 ml (20 fl oz/2½ cups) vegetable stock
9 teaspoons medium sherry

Chop onion, carrot and celery finely.

In a saucepan, heat oil for 1 minute. Add onion, carrot, celery and lentils and cook for 10 minutes, stirring. Stir in herbs, spices, salt and pepper, stock and sherry and mix well. Bring slowly to the boil, cover and simmer for 1 hour until the lentils are soft, stirring occasionally.

Remove pan from heat and set aside to cool. Once cool, purée the mixture in a blender or food processor until smooth. Return the sauce to a saucepan. Reheat gently and adjust the seasoning before serving. Serve with Middle Eastern dishes such as meatballs or kebabs.

Makes 850 ml (30 fl oz/3¾ cups/56 tbsp).

Calories per tablespoon: 17 Kcals/70 Kj
Fat per tablespoon: 0.3 g

—GREEN PEPPERCORN SAUCE—

15 g (½ oz/3 teaspoons) low fat spread
15 g (½ oz/6 teaspoons) plain flour
150 ml (5 fl oz/⅔ cup) vegetable stock
150 ml (5 fl oz/⅔ cup) semi-skimmed milk
1 tablespoon green peppercorns
25 g (1 oz/¼ cup) finely grated smoked hard cheese
salt and pepper

In a saucepan, melt low fat spread over a low heat. Whisk in flour and cook for 1 minute, whisking.

Remove pan from heat and gradually whisk in stock and milk. Bring slowly to the boil, whisking, and continue to cook until the mixture thickens. Simmer gently for 3 minutes. Remove pan from heat. Chop or crush the peppercorns.

Stir the peppercorns and cheese into the sauce, season with salt and pepper, and reheat gently, but do not allow the sauce to boil. Serve with lamb, pork or poultry.

Makes 350 ml (12 fl oz/1½ cups/23 tbsp).

Calories per tablespoon: 12 Kcals/50 Kj
Fat per tablespoon: 0.8 g

–HERBY YELLOW PEPPER SAUCE–

2 yellow peppers (capsicums)
½ green chilli
1 tablespoon chopped mixed fresh herbs, such as
    parsley, thyme, rosemary and chives
300 ml (10 fl oz/1¼ cups) vegetable stock
6 teaspoons medium white wine
salt and pepper
3 teaspoons cornflour

Seed and chop peppers (capsicums) and chilli finely. Put peppers (capsicums), chilli, herbs, stock, wine and salt and pepper into a saucepan and mix well.

Bring slowly to boil, cover and simmer gently for 10 minutes, stirring occasionally. Remove pan from heat and set aside to cool. Once cool, purée the mixture in a blender or food processor until smooth. Return sauce to a saucepan. In a small bowl, blend cornflour with 2 tablespoons water.

Stir cornflour mixture into pepper sauce and heat gently until sauce thickens, stirring continuously. Simmer gently for 3 minutes. Remove pan from heat and adjust the seasoning before serving. Serve with lamb or vegetables such as asparagus, broccoli or sweetcorn.

Makes 500 ml (18 fl oz/2¼ cups/33 tbsp).

Calories per tablespoon: 5 Kcals/21 Kj
Fat per tablespoon: 0.03 g

——TOMATO & BASIL SAUCE——

6 spring onions
1 clove garlic
2 teaspoons olive oil
450 g (1 lb) tomatoes
2 tablespoons chopped fresh basil
1 tablespoon tomato purée (paste)
½ teaspoon caster sugar
12 teaspoons medium sherry
salt and pepper

Chop spring onions finely and crush garlic. In a saucepan, heat oil for 1 minute. Add onions and garlic and cook for 5 minutes, stirring.

Peel and chop tomatoes finely and add to saucepan, mixing well. Stir the basil, tomato purée (paste), sugar, sherry and salt and pepper into the tomato mixture and mix well.

Bring slowly to the boil, cover and simmer for 20 minutes, stirring occasionally. Adjust the seasoning before serving. Serve with fresh filled pasta, such as tortellini or ravioli.

Makes 600 ml (21 fl oz/2¾ cups/40 tbsp).

Calories per tablespoon: 7 Kcals/31 Kj
Fat per tablespoon: 0.3 g

Variation: Use canned tomatoes in place of fresh tomatoes.

—PEA & SWEETCORN SAUCE—

1 onion
25 g (1 oz/6 teaspoons) low fat spread
350 g (12 oz) frozen peas
150 ml (5 fl oz/²⁄₃ cup) vegetable stock
½ teaspoon ground cumin
200 g (7 oz) can sweetcorn kernels
3 teaspoons sesame seeds
salt and pepper

Chop onion finely. In a saucepan, melt low fat spread over a low heat. Add onion and cook for 5 minutes, stirring. Stir in peas, stock and cumin, mixing well. Bring slowly to the boil, cover and simmer for 15 minutes.

Remove pan from heat and set aside to cool. Once cool, purée the mixture in a blender or food processor until smooth. Return the sauce to a saucepan. Drain sweetcorn and stir into the sauce.

Stir in sesame seeds and season with salt and pepper. Reheat the sauce gently and adjust the seasoning before serving. Serve with fish or poultry.

Makes 650 ml (23 fl oz/3 cups/43 tbsp).

Calories per tablespoon: 17 Kcals/70 Kj
Fat per tablespoon: 0.6 g

PIZZA SAUCE

1 onion
1 clove garlic
2 teaspoons olive oil
1 red pepper (capsicum)
175 g (6 oz) mushrooms
450 g (1 lb) tomatoes
1 tablespoon red wine vinegar
1 teaspoon caster sugar
1½ teaspoons dried basil
1½ teaspoons dried oregano
salt and pepper

Slice onion and crush garlic. In a saucepan, heat oil and cook onion and garlic for 3 minutes, stirring.

Seed and dice red pepper (capsicum), slice mushrooms, and peel and roughly chop the tomatoes. Add the pepper (capsicum), mushrooms, tomatoes and all the remaining ingredients to saucepan and mix well. Bring slowly to the boil, cover and simmer gently for 20 minutes, stirring occasionally.

Remove the cover and boil sauce rapidly for 10 minutes, to thicken it, stirring occasionally. Adjust the seasoning before serving. Serve as a topping on a pizza base.

Makes 800 ml (28 fl oz/3½ cups/53 tbsp).

Calories per tablespoon: 7 Kcals/31 Kj
Fat per tablespoon: 0.3 g

Variation: Add your own choice of chopped vegetables or chopped cooked meat to the basic pizza sauce recipe.

—CREAMY RED BEAN SAUCE—

1 small red onion
few sprigs parsley
few sprigs thyme
25 g (1 oz/6 teaspoons) low fat spread
two 400 g (14 oz) cans red kidney beans
150 ml (5 fl oz/²/₃ cup) vegetable stock
juice of 1 lemon
salt and pepper
12 teaspoons sour cream

Chop onion and herbs finely. In a saucepan, melt low fat spread over a low heat. Add onion and cook for 3 minutes, stirring.

Drain and rinse kidney beans. Stir kidney beans, stock, lemon juice, herbs and salt and pepper into saucepan, mixing well. Bring slowly to the boil, cover and simmer for 10 minutes, stirring occasionally. Remove pan from the heat and set aside to cool.

Once cool, purée the mixture in a blender or food processor until smooth. Return sauce to a saucepan and reheat gently. Adjust the seasoning and stir in the cream just before serving. Serve with meat or vegetables.

Makes 750 ml (26 fl oz/3¹/₂ cups/50 tbsp).

Calories per tablespoon: 21 Kcals/87 Kj
Fat per tablespoon: 0.5 g

Variation: Use other canned beans or pulses, such as chick peas, in place of kidney beans.

BLACK BEAN SAUCE

1 green chilli
4 spring onions
1 clove garlic
2.5 cm (1 in) piece fresh root ginger
2 teaspoons sesame oil
55 g (2 oz) fermented black beans
300 ml (10 fl oz/1¼ cups) vegetable stock
salt and pepper
3 teaspoons cornflour

Seed and chop chilli finely. Chop spring onions finely and crush garlic. Peel and chop ginger finely. In a saucepan, heat oil for 1 minute.

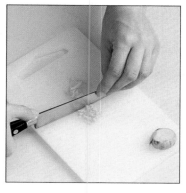

Add chilli, onions, garlic and ginger and cook for 5 minutes, stirring. Stir in beans, stock and salt and pepper and mix well. Bring slowly to the boil, cover and simmer for 10 minutes, stirring occasionally. In a small bowl, blend cornflour with 1 tablespoon water.

Stir cornflour mixture into the sauce and bring slowly to the boil, stirring continuously. Simmer gently for 3 minutes and adjust the seasoning before serving. Serve with Chinese dishes such as a stir-fry.

Makes 425 ml (15 fl oz/1¾ cups/28 tbsp).

Calories per tablespoon: 16 Kcals/67 Kj
Fat per tablespoon: 0.9 g

Note: Fermented black beans are available in Chinese supermarkets.

——FENNEL & OLIVE SAUCE——

2 bulbs fennel
25 g (1 oz/6 teaspoons) low fat spread
25 g (1 oz/¼ cup) plain flour
300 ml (10 fl oz/1¼ cups) semi-skimmed milk
20 black olives
1 teaspoon dried dill
salt and pepper

Trim and quarter fennel and cook in 300 ml (10 fl oz/1¼ cups) boiling water for 15-20 minutes until soft. Drain, reserving 150 ml (5 fl oz/⅔ cup) of the cooking liquid. Leave the cooked fennel aside to cool, then place in a blender or food processor with 3 tablespoons of the cooking liquid and purée until smooth.

In a saucepan, melt low fat spread over a low heat. Stir in flour and cook for 1 minute, stirring. Remove pan from heat and gradually stir or whisk in remaining cooking liquid and milk. Bring slowly to the boil, stirring or whisking and continue to cook until the mixture thickens. Simmer gently for 3 minutes. Stone and chop olives finely, then stir into the sauce with dill.

Stir in fennel purée and season with salt and pepper, mixing well. Reheat sauce gently and adjust the seasoning before serving. Serve with fish or poultry.

Makes 775 ml (27 fl oz/3½ cups/51 tbsp).

Calories per tablespoon: 10 Kcals/41 Kj
Fat per tablespoon: 0.5 g

—RATATOUILLE PASTA SAUCE—

1 onion
2 cloves garlic
3 teaspoons olive oil
1 aubergine (eggplant)
3 courgettes (zucchini)
1 green pepper (capsicum)
1 red pepper (capsicum)
400 g (14 oz) can chopped tomatoes
225 g (8 oz) can chopped tomatoes
1 tablespoon tomato purée (paste)
1 teaspoon dried basil
1 teaspoon dried oregano
salt and pepper

Slice onion and crush both cloves of garlic.

In a large saucepan, heat oil and cook onion and garlic for 3 minutes, stirring. Dice aubergine (eggplant), slice courgettes (zucchini), seed and slice peppers (capsicums) and add to saucepan.

Stir in tomatoes, tomato purée (paste), herbs and salt and pepper and mix well. Bring slowly to the boil, cover and simmer gently for 30 minutes, stirring occasionally. Adjust the seasoning before serving. Serve with freshly cooked pasta.

Serves 4.

Calories per serving: 127 Kcals/533 Kj
Fat per serving: 5.0 g

—SMOKED HAM & LEEK SAUCE—

225 g (8 oz) leeks
25 g (1 oz/6 teaspoons) low fat spread
25 g (1 oz/¼ cup) plain flour
425 ml (15 fl oz/1¾ cups) semi-skimmed milk
175 g (6 oz) cooked smoked ham
1 tablespoon chopped fresh chives
85 g (3 oz/¾ cup) reduced-fat Cheddar cheese
salt and pepper

Chop leeks finely. In a saucepan, melt low fat spread over a low heat. Add leeks and cook for 8-10 minutes until soft, stirring.

Stir in flour and cook for 1 minute, stirring. Remove pan from heat and gradually stir in milk. Bring slowly to the boil, stirring, and continue to cook until the mixture thickens. Simmer gently for 3 minutes. Remove pan from heat.

Chop ham finely and add to the sauce with the chives. Stir in cheese and salt and pepper and mix well. Reheat the sauce gently, stirring, but do not allow the sauce to boil. Serve with vegetables such as marrow, potatoes or broccoli.

Makes 850 ml (30 fl oz/3¾ cups/56 tbsp).

Calories per tablespoon: 15 Kcals/64 Kj
Fat per tablespoon: 0.7 g

Note: This makes a very thick sauce: add extra liquid if a thinner sauce is preferred.

—— BOLOGNESE PASTA SAUCE ——

1 onion
1 clove garlic
3 teaspoons sunflower oil
2 carrots
2 sticks celery
225 g (8 oz) mushrooms
55 g (2 oz) lean back bacon
450 g (1 lb) extra lean minced beef
400 g (14 oz) can chopped tomatoes
1 tablespoon tomato purée (paste)
150 ml (5 fl oz/⅔ cup) beef stock
150 ml (5 fl oz/⅔ cup) dry white wine
1 teaspoon dried mixed herbs
¼ teaspoon ground bay leaves or fresh bay leaves
salt and pepper

Chop onion and crush garlic. In a large sauce-pan, heat oil for 1 minute. Add onion and garlic and cook for 3 minutes, stirring. Chop carrots and celery finely and slice mush-rooms. Add to saucepan and cook for 5 minutes, stirring. Trim rind and fat from the bacon and chop bacon finely. Add bacon to saucepan with minced beef, mixing well. Cook until the meat is browned all over, stirring.

Stir in tomatoes, tomato purée (paste), stock, wine, herbs and salt and pepper and mix well. Bring slowly to the boil, cover and simmer for 1½-2 hours. Remove the cover for the last 30 minutes of the cooking time and increase the heat slightly, to thicken the sauce. Adjust the seasoning before serving. Serve with freshly cooked spaghetti or pasta shapes.

Serves 6.

Calories per serving: 207 Kcals/866 Kj
Fat per serving: 9.5 g

SEAFOOD SAUCE

1 small leek
2 cloves garlic
2 teaspoons olive oil
2 large tomatoes
150 ml (5 fl oz/²⁄₃ cup) fish stock
150 ml (5 fl oz/²⁄₃ cup) dry sherry
salt and pepper
16 shelled cooked mussels
115 g (4 oz) cooked peeled prawns
6 shelled oysters
225 g (8 oz) can crab meat, drained
3 teaspoons cornflour

Slice leek and crush cloves of garlic.

In a saucepan, heat oil for 1 minute. Add leeks and garlic and cook for 5 minutes, stirring. Peel and chop tomatoes and add to saucepan. Stir in stock, sherry and salt and pepper and mix well. Bring slowly to the boil, cover and simmer for 15-20 minutes, stirring occasionally. Stir in seafood. In a small bowl, blend the cornflour with 1 tablespoon cold water.

Stir the cornflour mixture into the sauce and bring slowly to the boil, stirring, until the mixture thickens. Simmer gently for 3 minutes. Remove the pan from the heat and adjust the seasoning before serving. Serve with pasta, rice or a selection of vegetables.

Makes 950 ml (33 fl oz/4¼ cups/63 tbsp).

Calories per tablespoon: 14 Kcals/59 Kj
Fat per tablespoon: 0.3 g

Note: Canned or bottled seafood may be used as an alternative to fresh seafood.

SHELLFISH PASTA SAUCE

1 bunch spring onions
2 cloves garlic
175 g (6 oz) button mushrooms
2 teaspoons olive oil
225 g (8 oz) shelled cooked mussels
225 g (8 oz) shelled cooked fresh clams
225 g (8 oz) shelled cooked fresh scallops
400 g (14 oz) can chopped tomatoes
150 ml (5 fl oz/²⁄₃ cup) dry white wine
finely grated rind of ½ lemon
salt and pepper
2 tablespoons chopped fresh parsley

Chop spring onions roughly and crush garlic.
Halve mushrooms, if preferred.

In a large saucepan, heat oil for 1 minute.
Add onions, garlic and mushrooms and cook
for 5 minutes, stirring. Add shellfish to the
pan. Stir in tomatoes, wine, lemon rind and
salt and pepper, mixing well. Bring slowly
to the boil, cover and simmer for 5-10
minutes, stirring occasionally.

Stir parsley into the sauce. Adjust the seasoning before serving. Serve with freshly cooked
pasta.

Serves 4.

Calories per serving: 252 Kcals/1059 Kj
Fat per serving: 5.4 g

Variation: Use any combination of shellfish
for this sauce.

SMOKED FISH SAUCE

350 g (12 oz) skinned smoked haddock fillets
300 ml (10 fl oz/1¼ cups) semi-skimmed milk
1 shallot
25 g (1 oz/6 teaspoons) low fat spread
25 g (1 oz/¼ cup) plain flour
115 g (4 oz) low fat soft cheese
1 tablespoon chopped fresh tarragon
salt and pepper

Place fish in a saucepan with the milk. Bring the milk slowly to the boil, cover and simmer for 15 minutes until fish is cooked.

Strain fish, reserving milk. Flake fish. Chop shallot finely. In a saucepan, melt low fat spread over a low heat. Add shallot and cook for 5 minutes, stirring. Stir or whisk in flour and cook for 1 minute, stirring. Remove pan from heat and gradually stir or whisk in reserved milk. Bring slowly to the boil, stirring or whisking, and continue to cook until the mixture thickens. Simmer gently for 3 minutes. Remove pan from heat and stir in the fish and soft cheese, mixing well.

Stir the tarragon into the sauce and season with salt and pepper. Reheat the sauce gently and adjust the seasoning before serving. Serve with vegetable dishes or eggs and slices of toast.

Makes 700 ml (24½ fl oz/3¼ cups/46 tbsp).

Calories per tablespoon: 19 Kcals/81 Kj
Fat per tablespoon: 0.8 g

Variation: Use other types of smoked fish, such as smoked mackerel, in place of the smoked haddock.

TUNA SAUCE

200 g (7 oz) can tuna in brine
115 g (4 oz) low fat soft cheese
150 ml (5 fl oz/²⁄₃ cup) low fat plain yogurt
1 tablespoon lemon juice
2 tablespoons chopped fresh parsley
salt and pepper

Drain and flake tuna fish into a bowl.

Stir soft cheese, plain yogurt, lemon juice, parsley and salt and pepper into the tuna and mix well. Leave the sauce in a cool place for 30 minutes before serving, to allow the flavours to develop.

Serve with cold cooked chicken, hard-boiled eggs, rice or pasta.

Makes 425 ml (15 fl oz/1¾ cups/28 tbsp).

Calories per tablespoon: 18 Kcals/75 Kj
Fat per tablespoon: 0.7 g

Variation: Use reduced fat single (light) cream in place of the yogurt, for a slightly richer sauce.

Calories per tablespoon: 21 Kcals/87 Kj
Fat per tablespoon: 1.1 g

——————— OYSTER SAUCE———————

25 g (1 oz/6 teaspoons) low fat spread
25 g (1 oz/¼ cup) plain flour
300 ml (10 fl oz/1¼ cups) fish stock
10 fresh oysters, cooked
1 tablespoon chopped fresh parsley
finely grated rind of ½ lemon
salt and pepper

In a saucepan, melt low fat spread over a low heat. Stir in flour and cook for 1 minute, stirring. Remove pan from heat and gradually whisk in fish stock. Bring slowly to the boil, whisking, and continue to cook until the mixture thickens.

Simmer gently for 3 minutes, then remove pan from heat. Open the oysters, remove from shells and chop roughly.

Stir oysters, parsley, lemon rind and salt and pepper into the sauce and reheat gently. Adjust the seasoning before serving. Serve with fish, pasta or rice.

Makes 300 ml (10 fl oz/1¼ cups/20 tbsp).

Calories per tablespoon: 15 Kcals/64 Kj
Fat per tablespoon: 0.6 g

Note: Canned oysters can be used in place of fresh oysters, if wished.

SALMON & COURGETTE SAUCE

1 small onion
1 small courgette (zucchini)
25 g (1 oz/6 teaspoons) low fat spread
25 g (1 oz/¼ cup) plain flour
300 ml (10 fl oz/1¼ cups) semi-skimmed milk
150 ml (5 fl oz/⅔ cup) fish stock
225 g (8 oz) can red salmon
1 teaspoon dried tarragon
¼ teaspoon ground nutmeg
few drops Tabasco sauce
salt and pepper

Chop onion and courgette (zucchini) finely. In a saucepan, melt low fat spread over a low heat.

Add onion and courgette (zucchini) and cook for 8-10 minutes until soft, stirring. Stir in flour and cook for 1 minute, stirring. Remove pan from heat and gradually stir in milk and stock. Bring slowly to the boil, stirring, and continue to cook until the mixture thickens. Simmer gently for 3 minutes.

Drain, bone and flake the salmon and stir into the sauce with tarragon, nutmeg, Tabasco and salt and pepper, mixing well. Reheat the sauce gently and adjust the seasoning before serving. Serve with pasta, rice or jacket potatoes.

Makes 700 ml (24½ fl oz/3¼ cups/46 tbsp).

Calories per tablespoon: 16 Kcals/67 Kj
Fat per tablespoon: 0.8 g

ANCHOVY SAUCE

55 g (2 oz) can anchovies
15 g (½ oz/3 teaspoons) low fat spread
15 g (½ oz/6 teaspoons) plain flour
300 ml (10 fl oz/1¼ cups) semi-skimmed milk
1 tablespoon lemon juice
salt and pepper

Chop anchovies finely and set aside. In a saucepan, melt low fat spread over a low heat. Stir in flour and cook for 1 minute, stirring. Remove pan from heat and gradually stir or whisk in milk.

Bring slowly to the boil, stirring or whisking, and continue to cook until the mixture thickens. Simmer gently for 3 minutes.

Add anchovies to the sauce with lemon juice and salt and pepper, mixing well. Reheat the sauce gently and adjust the seasoning before serving. Serve with fish or shellfish.

Makes 350 ml (12 fl oz/1½ cups/23 tbsp).

Calories per tablespoon: 23 Kcals/95 Kj
Fat per tablespoon: 1.6 g

CRANBERRY SAUCE

225 g (8 oz) cranberries
115 g (4 oz/½ cup) caster sugar
12 teaspoons ruby port

Place cranberries in a saucepan with 150 ml
(5 fl oz/⅔ cup) cold water.

Bring to the boil and boil rapidly until cranberries are soft. Reduce the heat and stir in
the sugar.

Heat gently until sugar has dissolved, then
stir in port. Reheat gently and serve with
turkey or pork.

Makes 450 ml (16 fl oz/2 cups/30 tbsp).

Calories per tablespoon: 19 Kcals/81 Kj
Fat per tablespoon: 0 g

Variation: In place of the ruby port, add
medium sherry to the sauce.

Calories per tablespoon: 19 Kcals/81 Kj
Fat per tablespoon: 0 g

AVOCADO SAUCE

2 ripe avocado pears
150 ml (5 fl oz/²/₃ cup) low fat plain yogurt
150 ml (5 fl oz/²/₃ cup) reduced calorie mayonnaise
1 teaspoon finely grated lemon rind
juice of 1 lemon
1 tablespoon chopped fresh parsley
salt and pepper

Peel, stone and chop avocado pears roughly.

Put avocados, yogurt, mayonnaise, lemon rind, lemon juice, parsley and salt and pepper into a blender or food processor. Blend the mixture until it is smooth. Put the sauce in a suitable serving dish and adjust the seasoning.

Stand the sauce in a cool place for 30 minutes before serving, to allow the flavours to develop. Serve with fish, poultry or reduced fat cheese.

Makes 600 ml (21 fl oz/2³/₄ cups/40 tbsp).

Calories per tablespoon: 26 Kcals/109 Kj
Fat per tablespoon: 2.5 g

Variation: Use reduced fat single (light) cream in place of the yogurt.

Calories per tablespoon: 29 Kcals/119 Kj
Fat per tablespoon: 2.8 g

BARBECUE SAUCE

2 garlic cloves
225 g (8 oz) can pineapple in fruit juice
225 g (8 oz) can chopped tomatoes
3 tablespoons cider vinegar
6 teaspoons soft brown sugar
6 teaspoons mango chutney
2 teaspoons Worcestershire sauce
½ teaspoon smooth mustard
½ teaspoon mixed spice
few drops Tabasco sauce
salt and pepper
3 teaspoons cornflour

Peel and crush garlic cloves and chop pineapple roughly.

Put garlic and pineapple in a saucepan with the tomatoes, vinegar, sugar, chutney, Worcestershire sauce, mustard, mixed spice, Tabasco sauce and salt and pepper and mix well. Bring slowly to the boil, cover and simmer gently for 10 minutes, stirring occasionally. Remove pan from heat and set aside to cool. Once cool, purée the sauce in a blender or food processor until smooth. Return the sauce to a saucepan.

In a small bowl, blend cornflour with 1 tablespoon water. Stir cornflour mixture into sauce and bring slowly to the boil, stirring continuously. Simmer gently for 3 minutes and adjust the seasoning before serving. Serve with barbecued or grilled meats such as steaks, chops or chicken portions.

Makes 400 ml (14 fl oz/1¾ cups/26 tbsp).

Calories per tablespoon: 14 Kcals/59 Kj
Fat per tablespoon: 0.1 g

SPICED APPLE SAUCE

450 g (1 lb) cooking apples
1 small onion
25 g (1 oz/6 teaspoons) low fat spread
25 g (1 oz/2 tablespoons) soft brown sugar
1 teaspoon mixed spice

Peel, core and slice apples thinly. Chop onion finely. Place apples in a saucepan with 2 tablespoons water. Cover saucepan and cook apples gently until they are soft.

Remove pan from heat and mash thoroughly with a fork or potato masher. In a separate saucepan, melt low fat spread over a low heat. Add onion and cook gently for 8-10 minutes until soft, stirring.

Stir in puréed apples, sugar and mixed spice, mixing well. Cook gently until sugar has dissolved. Serve hot or cold with pork, gammon or goose.

Makes 600 ml (21 fl oz/2¾ cups/40 tbsp).

Calories per tablespoon: 8 Kcals/34 Kj
Fat per tablespoon: 0.3 g

CUMBERLAND SAUCE

finely grated rind and juice of 1 orange
finely grated rind and juice of 1 lemon
12 teaspoons redcurrant jelly
2 tablespoons red wine vinegar
1 teaspoon smooth mustard
salt and pepper
3 teaspoons cornflour
12 teaspoons ruby port

Put orange rind and juice, lemon rind and juice, redcurrant jelly, red wine vinegar, mustard, salt and pepper and 4 tablespoons water in a bowl and mix well.

Pour mixture into a saucepan. Bring slowly to the boil, stirring. Cover and simmer for 5 minutes, stirring occasionally. In a small bowl, blend cornflour with 1 tablespoon water and port. Stir cornflour mixture into the sauce, mixing well.

Bring slowly to the boil, stirring continuously, until the mixture thickens. Simmer gently for 3 minutes. Remove pan from heat and adjust the seasoning before serving. Serve hot or cold with ham, pork, game or offal.

Makes 500 ml (18 fl oz/2¼ cups/33 tbsp).

Calories per tablespoon: 10 Kcals/41 Kj
Fat per tablespoon: 0.01 g

GOOSEBERRY SAUCE

450 g (1 lb) gooseberries
finely grated rind and juice of 1 orange
25 g (1 oz/6 teaspoons) low fat spread
25 g (1 oz/2 tablespoons) soft brown sugar
¼ teaspoon ground nutmeg

Place gooseberries in a saucepan with orange rind and juice and 150 ml (5 fl oz/⅔ cup) water, mixing well. Bring the mixture slowly to the boil, cover saucepan and simmer gently for 5-10 minutes until the gooseberries are cooked, stirring occasionally.

Remove the pan from the heat and set aside to cool. Once cool, purée the gooseberries in a blender or food processor until smooth. Return the mixture to a saucepan.

Stir in low fat spread, sugar and nutmeg. Bring slowly to the boil, stirring, and simmer gently for 1 minute. Serve with oily fish such as mackerel.

Makes 500 ml (18 fl oz/2¼ cups/33 tbsp).

Calories per tablespoon: 9 Kcals/36 Kj
Fat per tablespoon: 0.4 g

SWEET & SOUR SAUCE

225 g (8 oz) carrots
6 spring onions
1 clove garlic
2.5 cm (1 in) piece fresh root ginger
2 teaspoons olive oil
225 g (8 oz) unsweetened apple purée
450 ml (16 fl oz/2 cups) beef stock
150 ml (5 fl oz/⅔ cup) red wine
3 tablespoons lemon juice
6 teaspoons clear honey
6 teaspoons light soy sauce
salt and pepper
3 teaspoons cornflour

Grate carrots coarsely and chop onions finely. Peel and crush garlic. Peel and grate or chop ginger finely. In a saucepan, heat oil for 1 minute. Add carrots, spring onions, garlic and ginger and cook for 5 minutes, stirring. Stir in the apple purée, stock, red wine, lemon juice, honey, soy sauce and salt and pepper and mix well. Bring slowly to the boil, cover and simmer gently for 1 hour, stirring occasionally. Remove pan from heat and press the sauce through a nylon sieve. Discard pulp and return the sauce to a saucepan.

In a small bowl, blend cornflour with 1 tablespoon water. Stir cornflour mixture into sauce and bring slowly to the boil, stirring continuously. Simmer gently for 3 minutes and adjust the seasoning before serving. Serve with lamb, pork, fresh vegetables or mixed beans.

Makes 680 ml (24 fl oz/3 cups/45 tbsp).

Calories per tablespoon: 12 Kcals/50 Kj
Fat per tablespoon: 0.3 g

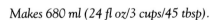

RHUBARB SAUCE

450 g (1 lb) rhubarb
225 g (8 oz) cooking apples
115 g (4 oz/½ cup) caster sugar
25 g (1 oz/6 teaspoons) low fat spread

Trim rhubarb and cut into 2.5 cm (1 in) slices. Peel, core and slice cooking apples thinly.

Place rhubarb and apples in a saucepan with 150 ml (5 fl oz/⅔ cup) water. Bring slowly to the boil, cover and simmer until fruit is soft and pulpy. Remove pan from heat and mash fruit thoroughly with a fork or potato masher.

Stir sugar and low fat spread into the rhubarb and mix well. Bring slowly to the boil and simmer gently for 1 minute, stirring. Serve the sauce hot or cold with oily fish such as mackerel.

Makes 850 ml (30 fl oz/3¾ cups/56 tbsp).

Calories per tablespoon: 12 Kcals/50 Kj
Fat per tablespoon: 0.2 g

FIG SAUCE

2 shallots or 1 onion
225 g (8 oz) dried figs
2 teaspoons olive oil
300 ml (10 fl oz/1¼ cups) chicken stock
2 tablespoons cider vinegar
1 tablespoon chopped fresh thyme
salt and pepper

Chop shallots or onion finely and chop figs roughly. In a saucepan, heat oil for 1 minute. Add shallots or onion and figs and cook for 5 minutes, stirring.

Stir in stock, vinegar, thyme and salt and pepper and mix well. Bring slowly to the boil, cover and simmer for 10 minutes, stirring occasionally. Remove pan from heat and set aside to cool.

Once cool, purée the mixture in a blender or food processor until smooth. Return sauce to a saucepan. Reheat gently and adjust the seasoning before serving. Serve hot or cold with lamb or beef.

Makes 500 ml (18 fl oz/2¼ cups/33 tbsp).

Calories per tablespoon: 18 Kcals/75 Kj
Fat per tablespoon: 0.4 g

─── PLUM SAUCE ───

350 g (12 oz) red dessert plums
finely grated rind and juice of 1 orange
55 g (2 oz/¼ cup) caster sugar
½ teaspoon ground cinnamon
3 teaspoons brandy

Halve and stone plums. Place plums in a saucepan with 150 ml (5 fl oz/⅔ cup) cold water.

Bring slowly to the boil, cover and simmer until the plums are soft. Remove pan from heat and set aside to cool. Once cool, purée the plums and juice in a blender or food processor until smooth.

Return the sauce to a saucepan and stir in orange rind, orange juice, sugar, cinnamon and brandy, mixing well. Reheat the sauce gently before serving. Serve with lamb, pork or beef.

Makes 550 ml (20 fl oz/2½ cups/36 tbsp).

Calories per tablespoon: 10 Kcals/41 Kj
Fat per tablespoon: 0.01 g

Note: The sauce may be served cold, if preferred.

— PINEAPPLE & ORANGE SAUCE —

300 g (10 oz) fresh pineapple
2 oranges
9 teaspoons apricot jam
1 teaspoon arrowroot
1 teaspoon mixed spice (optional)

Peel, core and chop pineapple roughly. Peel oranges and chop flesh roughly. Put pineapple, oranges and jam in a saucepan with 150 ml (5 fl oz/⅔ cup) water and mix well. Bring slowly to the boil, stirring. Cover and simmer gently for 15 minutes, stirring occasionally.

Remove pan from heat and set aside to cool. Once cool, purée the mixture in a blender or food processor until smooth. Strain the mixture through a nylon sieve, discarding the pulp. Return the sauce to a saucepan. Blend arrowroot with 1 tablespoon water.

Stir arrowroot mixture into the sauce. Bring slowly to the boil, stirring continuously until the sauce thickens. Stir in mixed spice, if using, before serving. Serve hot with chicken or turkey or serve cold with low fat ice cream or low fat yogurt.

Makes 450 ml (16 fl oz/2 cups/30 tbsp).

Calories per tablespoon: 12 Kcals/50 Kj
Fat per tablespoon: 0.03 g

—— MELON & GINGER SAUCE ——

1 canteloupe melon
85 g (3 oz) preserved stem ginger
150 ml (5 fl oz/⅔ cup) low fat plain yogurt
6 teaspoons syrup from ginger
3 teaspoons ginger wine

Peel and seed melon and chop flesh roughly.
Place melon in a blender or food processor
and blend until smooth.

Put puréed melon in a bowl. Chop ginger
finely and stir into melon, mixing well. Stir
in yogurt, ginger syrup and ginger wine and
mix well.

Cover and leave the sauce in a cool place for
at least 30 minutes before serving, to allow
the flavours to develop. Serve with fruit jelly
or fresh fruit.

Makes 700 ml (24½ fl oz/3¼ cups/46 tbsp).

Calories per tablespoon: 9 Kcals/36 Kj
Fat per tablespoon: 0.06 g

Variation: Use another type of melon such as
galia, ogen or charantais.

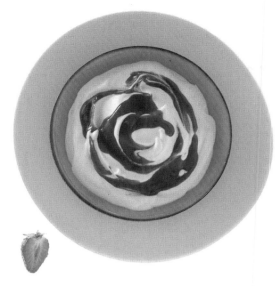

THICK FRUIT SAUCE

115 g (4 oz) plums
115 g (4 oz) raspberries
115 g (4 oz) strawberries
115 g (4 oz) blackberries
115 g (4 oz/1 cup) caster sugar
juice of 1 lime
2 teaspoons arrowroot

Halve and stone plums. Put plums, raspberries, strawberries and blackberries in a saucepan with 150 ml (5 fl oz/⅔ cup) water.

Bring slowly to the boil, cover and simmer gently until fruit is soft, stirring occasionally. Remove pan from the heat and set aside to cool. Once cool, purée the fruit in a blender or food processor until smooth. Return the sauce to a saucepan. Stir in sugar and lime juice and mix well. In a small bowl, blend arrowroot with 1 tablespoon water.

Stir arrowroot mixture into the sauce. Bring slowly to the boil, stirring continuously, until the sauce thickens. Serve hot or cold with low fat ice cream or frozen yogurt.

Makes 700 ml (24½ fl oz/3¼ cups/46 tbsp).

Calories per tablespoon: 13 Kcals/55 Kj
Fat per tablespoon: 0.01 g

Variation: Use any mixture of fruit of your choice.

──FRUITY YOGURT SAUCE──

300 g (10 oz) can mandarins in fruit juice
225 g (8 oz) can pineapple in fruit juice
300 ml (10 fl oz/1¼ cups) low fat plain yogurt
55 g (2 oz/⅓ cup) icing sugar

Put mandarins and pineapple and their juices in a blender or food processor and blend until smooth.

Put puréed fruit in a bowl. Stir in yogurt and mix well. Sift icing sugar.

Fold icing sugar gently into the fruit sauce, mixing well. Cover and leave the sauce in a cool place for 30 minutes before serving, to allow the flavours to develop. Serve with fresh fruit or baked puddings.

Makes 900 ml (32 fl oz/4 cups/60 tbsp).

Calories per tablespoon: 10 Kcals/41 Kj
Fat per tablespoon: 0.04 g

Variation: Use other canned fruits in fruit juices, for a different flavoured sauce.

–RASPBERRY & ALMOND SAUCE–

225 g (8 oz) raspberries
55 g (2 oz/¼ cup) caster sugar
150 ml (5 fl oz/⅔ cup) medium white wine
1 teaspoon arrowroot
few drops almond essence

Put raspberries in a saucepan with 2 table-spoons water. Bring slowly to the boil, cover and simmer gently until raspberries are soft. Remove pan from heat and set aside to cool. Once cool, purée the raspberries in a blender or food processor until smooth.

Press the purée through a nylon sieve and discard the pips. Return the sauce to a sauce-pan and stir in sugar and wine, mixing well. In a small bowl, blend arrowroot with 1 table-spoon water.

Stir the arrowroot mixture into the sauce. Bring slowly to the boil, stirring continu-ously, until the sauce thickens. Stir in a few drops of almond essence before serving. Serve hot or cold with baked puddings, low fat ice cream or fresh fruit.

Makes 300 ml (10 fl oz/1¼ cups/20 tbsp).

Calories per tablespoon: 20 Kcals/83 Kj
Fat per tablespoon: 0.03 g

—PEAR & RASPBERRY SAUCE—

225 g (8 oz) raspberries
400 g (14 oz) can pears in fruit juice
55 g (2 oz/¼ cup) caster sugar
6 teaspoons brandy
1 teaspoon arrowroot

Put raspberries, pears and pear juice in a blender or food processor. Blend the fruit until it is smooth.

Press fruit purée through a nylon sieve and discard pips. Put the fruit sauce in a saucepan. Stir in sugar and brandy and mix well.

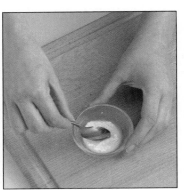

In a small bowl, blend arrowroot with 1 tablespoon water and stir into the sauce. Bring slowly to the boil, stirring continuously, until the sauce thickens. Serve hot or cold with mousses, crêpes or sponge pudding.

Makes 575 ml (21 fl oz/2½ cups/38 tbsp).

Calories per tablespoon: 13 Kcals/55 Kj
Fat per tablespoon: 0.02 g

Variation: Use peaches or pineapple in fruit juice in place of the pears.

SATSUMA SAUCE

10 satsumas
1 tablespoon lemon juice
55 g (2 oz/⅓ cup) soft brown sugar
2 teaspoons arrowroot
5 teaspoons Cointreau or orange liqueur

Peel and segment satsumas. Put satsumas in a saucepan with the lemon juice and 150 ml (5 fl oz/⅔ cup) water. Cover and cook gently until satsumas are soft, stirring occasionally.

Remove pan from heat and set aside to cool. Once cool, purée the mixture in a blender or food processor until smooth. Put the puréed satsumas in a saucepan with sugar and mix well. Heat the mixture gently until sugar has dissolved, stirring. In a small bowl, blend arrowroot with 1 tablespoon water until smooth. Stir arrowroot mixture into the fruit, mixing it in well.

Reheat gently until the sauce thickens, stirring continuously. Stir in Cointreau or orange liqueur and mix well. Serve with baked puddings or low fat cheesecakes.

Makes 550 ml (20 fl oz/2½ cups/36 tbsp).

Calories per tablespoon: 13 Kcals/55 Kj
Fat per tablespoon: 0.02 g

Note: Once the fruit has been puréed, strain the purée through a nylon sieve, if preferred.

CHOCOLATE SAUCE

3 teaspoons cocoa powder
6 teaspoons caster sugar
3 teaspoons cornflour
300 ml (10 fl oz/1¼ cups) semi-skimmed milk
15 g (½ oz/3 teaspoons) low fat spread

Sift cocoa powder into a bowl. Whisk in sugar, cornflour and a little milk and blend until smooth.

Put remaining milk and low fat spread in a saucepan and bring slowly to the boil. Remove pan from heat and pour the hot milk onto the blended cocoa mixture, whisking.

Return the sauce to the saucepan and reheat gently, stirring continuously, until the sauce thickens. Simmer gently for 3 minutes. Serve with custard puddings, profiteroles filled with low fat custard, canned or fresh fruit.

Makes 300 ml (10 fl oz/1¼ cups/20 tbsp).

Calories per tablespoon: 21 Kcals/87 Kj
Fat per tablespoon: 0.7 g

BRANDY SAUCE

6 teaspoons cornflour
300 ml (10 fl oz/1¼ cups) semi-skimmed milk
6 teaspoons caster sugar
9 teaspoons brandy

In a bowl, blend cornflour with 2 tablespoons milk until smooth. Put remaining milk in a saucepan and bring slowly to the boil.

Pour hot milk onto cornflour mixture, whisking. Return the sauce to the saucepan and bring slowly to the boil, stirring continuously, until the sauce thickens. Simmer gently for 3 minutes.

Remove pan from heat and stir in sugar and brandy. Reheat the sauce gently. Serve with Christmas pudding or mince pies.

Makes 300 ml (10 fl oz/1¼ cups/20 tbsp).

Calories per tablespoon: 23 Kcals/95 Kj
Fat per tablespoon: 0.3 g

Variation: Replace the brandy with rum, sherry or whisky.

CARAMEL SAUCE

115 g (4 oz/³⁄₄ cup) soft brown sugar
115 g (4 oz/¹⁄₂ cup) caster sugar
3 teaspoons arrowroot

Put sugars in a saucepan with 450 ml (16 fl oz/ 2 cups) water. Heat mixture gently until sugar has dissolved. Bring slowly to the boil and simmer gently for 10 minutes, stirring occasionally.

In a small bowl, blend arrowroot with 2 table-spoons water. Whisk arrowroot mixture into sugar, mixing well. Reheat the sauce gently, until sauce thickens, stirring continuously.

Serve with fruit such as oranges or bananas.

Makes 425 ml (15 fl oz/1³⁄₄ cups/28 tbsp).

Calories per tablespoon: 34 Kcals/146 Kj
Fat per tablespoon: 0 g

Variation: Once the sauce has thickened, add 2-3 tablespoons brandy or a liqueur such as Cointreau to the sauce and reheat gently.

Calories per tablespoon: 38 Kcals/161 Kj
Fat per tablespoon: 0 g

CUSTARD SAUCE

3 teaspoons caster sugar
3 teaspoons cornflour
pinch of salt
2 egg yolks
300 ml (10 fl oz/1 ¼ cups) semi-skimmed milk
few drops vanilla essence

Put sugar, cornflour, salt and egg yolks in a
bowl. Add 2 tablespoons of milk and whisk
until smooth. In a saucepan, bring remaining
milk slowly to the boil.

Pour hot milk onto cornflour mixture, whisking well. Return mixture to the saucepan and
bring slowly to the boil, whisking continuously, until the mixture thickens.

Simmer gently for 1 minute. Whisk in a few
drops of vanilla essence before serving. Serve
with baked apples, canned or fresh fruit.

Makes 300 ml (10 fl oz/1 ¼ cups/20 tbsp).

Calories per tablespoon: 19 Kcals/81 Kj
Fat per tablespoon: 0.9 g

MELBA SAUCE

450 g (1 lb) raspberries
115 g (4 oz/³⁄₄ cup) icing sugar
9 teaspoons medium white wine
1 teaspoon arrowroot

Put raspberries in a saucepan with 2 table-spoons water. Cover and cook raspberries gently until they are soft. Remove pan from heat and set aside to cool.

Once cool, strain raspberries through a nylon sieve, discarding pips. Sift icing sugar and place in saucepan with raspberry sauce and wine, mixing well. Heat the sauce gently until sugar has dissolved, then bring to the boil. Remove pan from heat. In a small bowl, blend arrowroot with 1 tablespoon water.

Stir arrowroot mixture into raspberry sauce. Reheat gently until sauce thickens, stirring continuously. Serve hot or cold with peaches, low fat ice cream or sorbet.

Makes 535 ml (19 fl oz/2¹⁄₃ cups/35 tbsp).

Calories per tablespoon: 18 Kcals/75 Kj
Fat per tablespoon: 0.04 g

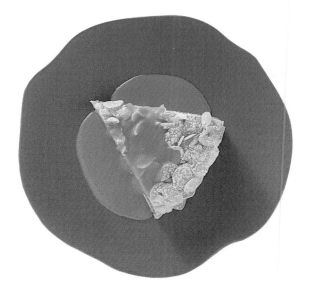

COFFEE SAUCE

4 teaspoons cornflour
300 ml (10 fl oz/1¼ cups) semi-skimmed milk
2 teaspoons instant coffee powder
6 teaspoons caster sugar

In a bowl, blend cornflour with 2 tablespoons milk until smooth. In a saucepan, bring remaining milk slowly to the boil.

Pour the hot milk onto cornflour mixture, stirring. Return sauce to a saucepan and bring slowly to the boil, stirring continuously, until mixture thickens. Simmer gently for 3 minutes. Remove pan from heat. Dissolve coffee powder in 2 tablespoons hot water.

Stir coffee and sugar into sauce and reheat gently before serving. Serve with stewed fruit, frozen yogurt or low calorie pies.

Makes 400 ml (14 fl oz/1¾ cups/26 tbsp).

Calories per tablespoon: 13 Kcals/55 Kj
Fat per tablespoon: 0.2 g

APRICOT SAUCE

225 g (8 oz) dried apricots
55 g (2 oz/¼ cup) caster sugar
300 ml (10 fl oz/1¼ cups) dry white wine

Chop apricots roughly. Place sugar in a sauce-pan with 150 ml (5 fl oz/⅔ cup) water. Heat mixture gently until sugar has dissolved.

Stir in apricots and wine, mixing well. Bring slowly to the boil, cover and simmer gently for 20 minutes, stirring occasionally. Remove pan from heat and set aside to cool.

Once cool, purée the mixture in a blender or food processor until smooth. Return the sauce to a saucepan and reheat gently before serving. Serve with baked puddings, crêpes or baked fruit such as baked pears.

Makes 550 ml (20 fl oz/2½ cups/36 tbsp).

Calories per tablespoon: 21 Kcals/87 Kj
Fat per tablespoon: 0.04 g

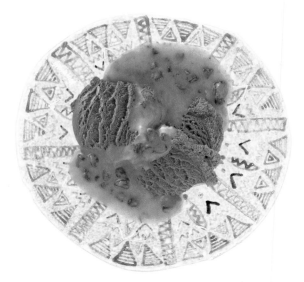

——— RUM & RAISIN SAUCE ———

25 g (1 oz/3 tablespoons) cornflour
25 g (1 oz/5 teaspoons) caster sugar
450 ml (16 fl oz/2 cups) semi-skimmed milk
85 g (3 oz/½ cup) raisins
12 teaspoons rum
6 teaspoons reduced fat single (light) cream

In a bowl or jug, blend cornflour and sugar with 2 tablespoons milk until smooth. In a saucepan, bring remaining milk slowly to the boil. Pour the hot milk onto cornflour mixture, stirring, and return mixture to the saucepan.

Reheat gently until sauce thickens, stirring continuously. Simmer gently for 3 minutes, then remove pan from heat. Chop raisins roughly and stir into sauce.

Stir in rum and cream. Reheat the sauce very gently, but do not allow the sauce to boil. Serve with pancakes or low fat ice cream.

Makes 550 ml (20 fl oz/2½ cups/36 tbsp).

Calories per tablespoon: 22 Kcals/93 Kj
Fat per tablespoon: 0.3 g

LEMON SAUCE

300 ml (10 fl oz/1¼ cups) low fat plain yogurt
115 g (4 oz) low fat soft cheese
55 g (2 oz/⅓ cup) icing sugar
finely grated rind and juice of 2 lemons

In a bowl, whisk together yogurt and soft cheese. Sift icing sugar and stir into yogurt mixture, mixing well.

Stir in lemon rind and lemon juice and mix thoroughly. Cover and leave the sauce in a cool place for 30 minutes before serving, to allow the flavours to develop.

Serve with sponge puddings or fresh fruit compote.

Makes 500 ml (18 fl oz/2¼ cups/33 tbsp).

Calories per tablespoon: 18 Kcals/75 Kj
Fat per tablespoon: 0.6 g

Variation: Use the finely grated rind and juice of 2 small oranges in place of the lemons. You could also use a mixture of fruit such as 1 lemon and 1 orange, or 1 lemon and 1 lime.

——— RASPBERRY & FIG SAUCE ———

225 g (8 oz) dried figs
400 g (14 oz) can raspberries in fruit juice
55 g (2 oz/¼ cup) caster sugar
6 teaspoons brandy or raspberry liqueur

Chop figs roughly. Put figs, raspberries and juice in a bowl with 150 ml (5 fl oz/⅔ cup) water and mix well. Cover and leave to soak in a cool place overnight.

Purée mixture in a blender or food processor until smooth.

Put the sauce in a saucepan and stir in sugar and brandy or liqueur. Bring slowly to the boil and simmer for 1 minute. Serve with mousses, moulded desserts, baked puddings or crêpes.

Makes 700 ml (24½ fl oz/3¼ cups/46 tbsp).

Calories per tablespoon: 25 Kcals/106 Kj
Fat per tablespoon: 0.09 g

Note: Once the sauce has been puréed, strain the sauce through a nylon sieve to remove the seeds and pips, if preferred.

SWEET SHERRY SAUCE

5 teaspoons cornflour
300 ml (10 fl oz/1¼ cups) semi-skimmed milk
5 teaspoons caster sugar
9 teaspoons sweet sherry

In a bowl, blend cornflour with 2 tablespoons milk until smooth. In a saucepan, bring remaining milk slowly to the boil.

Remove pan from heat and pour the hot milk onto cornflour mixture, stirring. Return mixture to the saucepan and reheat gently until mixture thickens, stirring continuously.

Remove pan from heat and stir in sugar and sherry, mixing well. Reheat the sauce gently before serving. Serve with steamed or baked fruit puddings.

Makes 350 ml (12 fl oz/1½ cups/23 tbsp).

Calories per tablespoon: 17 Kcals/70 Kj
Fat per tablespoon: 0.2 g

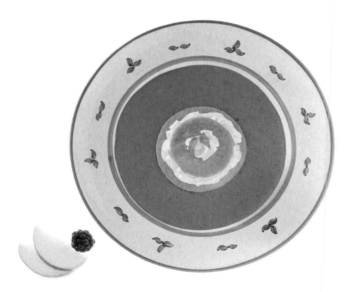

—BLACKBERRY & APPLE SAUCE—

225 g (8 oz) cooking apples
225 g (8 oz) blackberries
55 g (2 oz/¼ cup) caster sugar
115 g (4 oz) low fat soft cheese
150 ml (5 fl oz/⅔ cup) reduced fat single (light) cream

Peel, core and slice apples thinly. Put apples and blackberries in a saucepan with 3 table-spoons water. Cover and cook gently until fruit is soft, stirring occasionally.

Remove pan from heat and stir in sugar. Set aside to cool. Once cool, purée the fruit in a blender or food processor until smooth. Press the fruit through a nylon sieve, discarding pips.

Whisk soft cheese and cream together, then whisk fruit in, mixing thoroughly. Serve with steamed and baked puddings, meringues or poached fruit such as peaches or pears.

Makes 550 ml (20 fl oz/2½ cups/36 tbsp).

Calories per tablespoon: 20 Kcals/83 Kj
Fat per tablespoon: 0.9 g

Variation: In place of blackberries, use raspberries, loganberries or blackcurrants.

MADEIRA SAUCE

115 g (4 oz/¾ cup) soft brown sugar
9 teaspoons brandy
55g (2 oz/¼ cup) low fat spread
150 ml (5 fl oz/⅔ cup) Madeira
3 teaspoons arrowroot

Put sugar and brandy in a saucepan with 300 ml (10 fl oz/1¼ cups) water. Heat gently, stirring, until sugar has dissolved.

Stir in low fat spread and Madeira and bring slowly to the boil, whisking continuously. Remove pan from heat. In a small bowl, blend arrowroot with 2 tablespoons water until smooth.

Stir arrowroot mixture into the sauce, mixing well. Reheat the sauce gently, stirring continuously, until sauce thickens. Serve with steamed or baked fruit puddings or low fat ice cream.

Makes 800 ml (28 fl oz/3½ cups/53 tbsp).

Calories per tablespoon: 20 Kcals/83 Kj
Fat per tablespoon: 0.4 g

MANGO SAUCE

1 mango
45 g (1½ oz/3 tablespoons) low fat spread
55 g (2 oz/½ cup) plain flour
450 ml (16 fl oz/2 cups) semi-skimmed milk
55 g (2 oz/⅓ cup) soft brown sugar

Peel and stone mango and chop flesh roughly. Place mango in a blender or food processor and blend until smooth. Set aside. In a saucepan, melt low fat spread over a low heat. Stir in flour and cook for 1 minute, stirring.

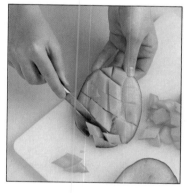

Remove pan from heat and gradually whisk in the milk. Bring slowly to the boil, whisking, and continue to cook until mixture thickens. Simmer gently for 3 minutes.

Remove pan from heat and stir in puréed mango and sugar, mixing well. Reheat the sauce gently before serving. Serve with tropical fresh fruit salad or fruit compote.

Makes 700 ml (24½ fl oz/3¼ cups/46 tbsp).

Calories per tablespoon: 20 Kcals/83 Kj
Fat per tablespoon: 0.6 g

GINGER SAUCE

55 g (2 oz/¼ cup) caster sugar
55 g (2 oz) preserved stem ginger
12 teaspoons syrup from stem ginger
2 tablespoons lemon juice
1 teaspoon arrowroot

Put sugar in a saucepan with 150 ml (5 fl oz/ ⅔ cup) water. Heat gently until sugar has dissolved, stirring, then bring to the boil and boil for 5 minutes.

Chop stem ginger finely and stir into sugar mixture with ginger syrup and lemon juice, mixing well. In a small bowl, blend arrowroot with 1 tablespoon water until smooth.

Stir arrowroot mixture into the sauce. Reheat gently, stirring continuously, until sauce thickens. Serve with fresh melon, fresh fruit salad or hot steamed puddings.

Makes 225 ml (8 fl oz/¾ cup/15 tbsp).

Calories per tablespoon: 29 Kcals/121 Kj
Fat per tablespoon: 0.02 g

MIXED BERRY SAUCE

115 g (4 oz) raspberries
115 g (4 oz) blackberries
115 g (4 oz) gooseberries
9 teaspoons clear honey
1 teaspoon mixed spice

Put raspberries, blackberries and gooseberries in a saucepan with 3 tablespoons water. Cover and cook gently until fruit is soft, stirring occasionally. Remove pan from heat and set aside to cool.

Once cool, purée the fruit in a blender or food processor until smooth. Press the fruit purée through a nylon sieve and discard pips.

Put the fruit sauce in a saucepan and stir in honey and spice, mixing well. Reheat the sauce gently, stirring. Serve hot or cold with pancakes, summer pudding or baked puddings.

Makes 300 ml (10 fl oz/1¼ cups/20 tbsp).

Calories per tablespoon: 10 Kcals/41 Kj
Fat per tablespoon: 0.06 g

Variation: Use any mixture of fruit of your choice.

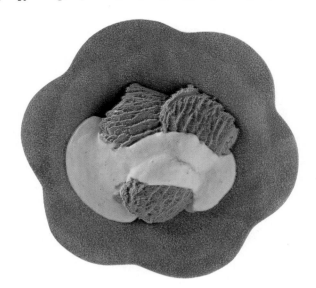

—BANANA & GINGER SAUCE—

3 bananas, approximately 450 g (1 lb) in weight
juice of 1 lemon
juice of 1 lime
450 ml (16 fl oz/2 cups) low fat plain yogurt
12 teaspoons soft brown sugar
2 teaspoons ground ginger

Peel and slice bananas. Put bananas, lemon juice and lime juice in a blender or food processor and blend until smooth.

Add yogurt, sugar and ginger to the blender or food processor and blend mixture until thoroughly mixed.

Pour sauce into a suitable serving dish, cover and leave the sauce in a cool place for 30 minutes before serving, to allow the flavours to develop. Serve with fresh fruit, low fat ice cream or frozen yogurt.

Makes 700 ml (24½ fl oz/3¼ cups/46 tbsp).

Calories per tablespoon: 17 Kcals/70 Kj
Fat per tablespoon: 0.1 g

-STRAWBERRY & LEMON SAUCE -

225 g (8 oz) strawberries
finely grated rind and juice of 2 lemons
55 g (2 oz/¼ cup) caster sugar
1 teaspoon arrowroot

Put strawberries in a blender or food processor and blend until smooth. Set aside. Pour into a saucepan.

Add 150 ml (5 fl oz/⅔ cup) water to the saucepan and stir in lemon rind, lemon juice and sugar. Heat gently, stirring, until sugar has dissolved, then bring mixture to the boil and simmer gently for 5 minutes. In a small bowl, blend arrowroot with 1 tablespoon water until smooth.

Stir arrowroot mixture into the saucepan, mixing well. Reheat the sauce gently until mixture thickens, stirring continuously. Serve with fruit jelly, fresh fruit, fruit tart or sorbet.

Makes 450 ml (16 fl oz/2 cups/30 tbsp).

Calories per tablespoon: 10 Kcals/41 Kj
Fat per tablespoon: 0.008 g

—VANILLA YOGURT SAUCE—

150 ml (5 fl oz/²⁄₃ cup) semi-skimmed milk
1 vanilla pod
1 teaspoon cornflour
55 g (2 oz/¹⁄₃ cup) icing sugar
300 ml (10 fl oz/1¹⁄₄ cups) low fat plain yogurt

In a saucepan, warm milk. Split vanilla pod lengthways and add to milk. Remove pan from heat, cover and set aside to infuse for 15 minutes.

Remove vanilla pod and scrape seeds from pod into milk. In a small bowl, blend cornflour with 1 tablespoon water until smooth. Stir cornflour mixture into milk and bring slowly to the boil, stirring continuously, until mixture thickens. Simmer sauce gently for 3 minutes, stirring.

Remove pan from heat, pour sauce into a bowl and set aside to cool. Sift icing sugar into a bowl. Once the cornflour sauce is cool, stir in the icing sugar and yogurt and mix thoroughly. Serve with hot or cold puddings or meringues.

Makes 430 ml (15 fl oz/1¾ cups/28 tbsp).

Calories per tablespoon: 17 Kcals/70 Kj
Fat per tablespoon: 0.2 g

BLACKCURRANT SAUCE

225 g (8 oz) blackcurrants
9 teaspoons clear honey
6 teaspoons blackcurrant liqueur, such as Cassis
1 teaspoon arrowroot

Top and tail blackcurrants and place in a saucepan with honey and 4 tablespoons water. Cover and cook mixture gently until blackcurrants are soft, stirring occasionally.

Remove pan from heat and stir in blackcurrant liqueur. In a small bowl, blend arrowroot with 1 tablespoon water until smooth. Stir arrowroot mixture into blackcurrants and mix well.

Bring slowly to the boil, stirring continuously, until sauce thickens. Serve hot or cold with frozen yogurt or fresh fruit such as figs.

Makes 450 ml (16 fl oz/2 cups/30 tbsp).

Calories per tablespoon: 9 Kcals/36 Kj
Fat per tablespoon: 0 g

KIWI & LIME SAUCE

8 ripe kiwi fruit, approximately 450 g (1 lb) in weight
finely grated rind and juice of 1 lime
115 g (4 oz) low fat soft cheese
150 ml (5 fl oz/²/₃ cup) reduced fat single (light) cream
55 g (2 oz/¹/₃ cup) icing sugar

Peel and quarter kiwi fruit. Put kiwi fruit, lime rind and lime juice in a blender or food processor and blend until smooth.

Add soft cheese and cream to the blender or food processor and blend until thoroughly mixed. Pour sauce into a bowl.

Sift icing sugar and stir into sauce, mixing well. Cover and leave the sauce to stand in a cool place for 30 minutes before serving, to allow the flavours to develop. Serve with low fat ice cream, sorbet or fresh fruit salad.

Makes 725 ml (25½ fl oz/3¼ cups/48 tbsp).

Calories per tablespoon: 17 Kcals/70 Kj
Fat per tablespoon: 0.7 g

SWEET CHERRY NUTMEG SAUCE

350 g (12 oz) dessert cherries
9 teaspoons bramble jelly
150 ml (5 fl oz/⅔ cup) low fat plain yogurt
2 teaspoons ground nutmeg

Stone cherries and chop them roughly. Put cherries in a saucepan with bramble jelly and 4 tablespoons water.

Cook mixture gently, stirring, until jelly has dissolved. Cover and continue cooking gently for 10 minutes until cherries are soft, stirring occasionally. Remove pan from heat, pour mixture into a bowl and set aside to cool.

Once cool, stir in yogurt and nutmeg and mix thoroughly. Serve with fresh fruit, crêpes or low fat ice cream.

Makes 450 ml (16 fl oz/2 cups/30 tbsp).

Calories per tablespoon: 11 Kcals/47 Kj
Fat per tablespoon: 0.2 g

Variation: For a richer sauce, replace the yogurt with reduced fat single (light) cream.

Calories per tablespoon: 15 Kcals/64 Kj
Fat per tablespoon: 0.6 g

– COCONUT YOGURT DRESSING –

300 ml (10 fl oz/1 ¼ cups) low fat plain yogurt
6 tablespoons desiccated coconut
6 teaspoons clear honey
juice of 1 lime

Put yogurt and desiccated coconut in a bowl and mix well.

Whisk in honey and lime juice, mixing well. Cover and leave the dressing in a cool place for 30 minutes before serving, to allow the flavours to develop.

Serve with a bean salad or a mixed salad.

Makes 400 ml (14 fl oz/1¾ cups/26 tbsp).

Calories per tablespoon: 31 Kcals/128 Kj
Fat per tablespoon: 2.2 g

Variation: For a special dressing, add 6 tea-spoons coconut liqueur, such as Malibu, to the dressing with the honey.

Calories per tablespoon: 33 Kcals/138 Kj
Fat per tablespoon: 2.2 g

TARTARE SAUCE

55 g (2 oz) gherkins
1 tablespoon capers
300 ml (10 fl oz/1¼ cups) reduced calorie mayonnaise
1 tablespoon tarragon vinegar
1 tablespoon chopped fresh parsley
1 tablespoon chopped fresh chives
2 teaspoons chopped fresh tarragon
salt and pepper

Using a sharp knife, chop gherkins and capers finely.

Put gherkins and capers in a bowl and stir in the mayonnaise, mixing well.

Stir in vinegar, parsley, chives, tarragon and salt and pepper and mix thoroughly. Cover and leave in a cool place for at least 30 minutes before serving, to allow the flavours to develop. Serve with grilled or baked fish.

Makes 400 ml (14 fl oz/1¾ cups/26 tbsp).

Calories per tablespoon: 34 Kcals/139 Kj
Fat per tablespoon: 3 g

– THOUSAND ISLAND DRESSING –

55 g (2 oz) gherkins
2 tablespoons chopped red pepper (capsicum)
2 tablespoons chopped green pepper (capsicum)
300 ml (10 fl oz/1 ¼ cups) reduced calorie mayonnaise
4 tablespoons low fat plain yogurt
6 teaspoons tomato ketchup (sauce)
1 tablespoon chopped fresh parsley
salt and pepper

Chop gherkins finely. In a bowl, mix together gherkins and red and green pepper (capsicum).

Stir in mayonnaise, yogurt, tomato ketchup (sauce), parsley and salt and pepper and mix thoroughly. Cover and leave in a cool place for 30 minutes before serving, to allow the flavours to develop.

Serve with a fresh mixed seafood salad.

Makes 600 ml (21 fl oz/2¾ cups/40 tbsp).

Calories per tablespoon: 24 Kcals/98 Kj
Fat per tablespoon: 2.1 g

Variation: Add two cold hard-boiled eggs, mashed or finely chopped, to the dressing.

Calories per tablespoon: 29 Kcals/121 Kj
Fat per tablespoon: 2.5 g

——MILD CURRY MAYONNAISE——

6 spring onions
15 g (½ oz/3 teaspoons) low fat spread
6 teaspoons mango chutney
3 teaspoons mild curry powder
3 teaspoons desiccated coconut
300 ml (10 fl oz/1¼ cups) reduced calorie mayonnaise
150 ml (5 fl oz/⅔ cup) low fat plain yogurt
salt and pepper

Trim and chop spring onions finely. In a saucepan, melt low fat spread over a low heat. Add spring onions and cook for 5 minutes, stirring.

Remove pan from heat and stir in chutney, curry powder and coconut, mixing well. Set aside to cool.

Once cool, mix with mayonnaise, yogurt and salt and pepper. Cover and leave the sauce in a cool place for 30 minutes before serving, to allow the flavours to develop. Serve with potato salad or coleslaw.

Makes 500 ml (18 fl oz/2¼ cups/33 tbsp).

Calories per tablespoon: 36 Kcals/147 Kj
Fat per tablespoon: 3 g

HOT CHILLI DRESSING

1 clove garlic
½ red chilli
12 teaspoons olive oil
6 tablespoons cider vinegar
150 ml (5 fl oz/⅔ cup) tomato juice
6 teaspoons tomato ketchup (sauce)
2 teaspoons smooth mustard
few drops Tabasco sauce
salt and pepper

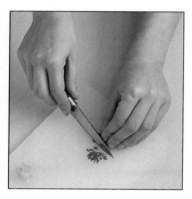

Peel and crush garlic. Seed and chop chilli finely.

Put garlic, chilli, olive oil, vinegar, tomato juice, tomato ketchup (sauce), mustard, Tabasco sauce and salt and pepper in a bowl.

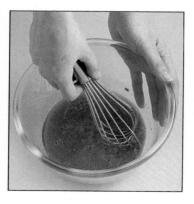

Whisk the ingredients together until thoroughly mixed. Adjust the seasoning before serving. Serve with a seafood or rice salad.

Makes 400 ml (14 fl oz/1¾ cups/26 tbsp).

Calories per tablespoon: 24 Kcals/98 Kj
Fat per tablespoon: 2.3 g

Note: Instead of whisking the ingredients together in a bowl, put all the ingredients in a clean jam jar, screw the top on and shake until all the ingredients are well mixed.

FRENCH DRESSING

12 teaspoons olive oil
4 tablespoons white wine vinegar
4 tablespoons tarragon vinegar
150 ml (5 fl oz/²⁄₃ cup) white grape juice
2 teaspoons chopped fresh mixed herbs, such as
    parsley, thyme, mint and rosemary
2 teaspoons wholegrain mustard
pinch caster sugar
salt and pepper

Put olive oil, vinegars, grape juice, herbs, mustard, sugar and salt and pepper in a bowl. Whisk ingredients together until thoroughly mixed.

Alternatively, put all the ingredients in a clean jam jar. Screw top on jar and shake until ingredients are thoroughly mixed.

Adjust seasoning before serving. Serve with a fresh mixed salad or a selection of raw or cooked vegetables.

Makes 325 ml (11 fl oz/1¹⁄₃ cups/21 tbsp).

Calories per tablespoon: 31 Kcals/128 Kj
Fat per tablespoon: 2.9 g

WALNUT DRESSING

1 clove garlic
12 teaspoons walnut oil
3 tablespoons red wine vinegar
3 tablespoons cider vinegar
150 ml (5 fl oz/²⁄₃ cup) red grape juice
1 tablespoon chopped fresh parsley
1 teaspoon French mustard
pinch caster sugar
salt and pepper

Peel and crush garlic, then put garlic, oil, vinegars, grape juice, parsley, mustard, sugar and salt and pepper in a bowl.

Whisk ingredients together until thoroughly mixed. Alternatively, put all ingredients in a clean jam jar. Screw top on jar and shake until ingredients are thoroughly mixed.

Adjust the seasoning before serving. Serve the dressing with a mixed bean salad or cooked vegetables.

Makes 350 ml (12 fl oz/1½ cups/23 tbsp).

Calories per tablespoon: 28 Kcals/114 Kj
Fat per tablespoon: 2.6 g

—— SWEET & SOUR DRESSING ——

1 clove garlic
2.5 cm (1 in) piece fresh root ginger
12 teaspoons olive oil
5 tablespoons lemon juice
5 tablespoons red wine vinegar
6 teaspoons clear honey
6 teaspoons light soy sauce
6 teaspoons tomato ketchup (sauce)
6 teaspoons medium sherry
3 teaspoons sesame seeds
pinch cayenne pepper
salt and pepper

Peel and crush garlic. Peel and chop or grate ginger finely.

Put garlic, ginger, oil, lemon juice, vinegar, honey, soy sauce, tomato ketchup (sauce), sherry, sesame seeds, cayenne pepper and salt and pepper in a bowl. Whisk ingredients together until thoroughly mixed.

Alternatively, put all ingredients in a clean jam jar. Screw top on jar and shake until ingredients are thoroughly mixed. Adjust the seasoning before serving. Serve with fresh salad leaves, seafood salad or chicken salad.

Makes 350 ml (12 fl oz/1½ cups/23 tbsp).

Calories per tablespoon: 35 Kcals/143 Kj
Fat per tablespoon: 3 g

——HERBY CHEESE DRESSING——

1 clove garlic
225 g (8 oz) low fat soft cheese
150 ml (5 fl oz/⅔ cup) sour cream
2 tablespoons chopped fresh mixed herbs, such as
    parsley, chives, rosemary and thyme
1 tablespoon lemon juice
salt and pepper

Peel and crush garlic. Put garlic, soft cheese, cream, herbs, lemon juice and salt and pepper in a bowl.

Whisk ingredients together until thoroughly mixed. Cover and leave the dressing in a cool place for 30 minutes before serving, to allow the flavours to develop.

Adjust the seasoning before serving. Serve with fresh salad leaves, raw or cooked vegetables, pasta salad or beef salad.

Makes 350 ml (12 fl oz/1½ cups/23 tbsp).

Calories per tablespoon: 31 Kcals/128 Kj
Fat per tablespoon: 2.7 g

— TOMATO YOGURT DRESSING —

1 shallot
225 g (8 oz) tomatoes
15 g (½ oz/3 teaspoons) low fat spread
300 ml (10 fl oz/1¼ cups) low fat plain yogurt
2 tablespoons chopped fresh basil
salt and pepper

Chop shallot finely. Peel and chop tomatoes finely. In a saucepan, melt low fat spread over a low heat.

Add shallot and tomatoes and cook for 5-10 minutes until soft, stirring. Remove pan from heat and set aside to cool.

In a bowl, stir together cooled tomato mixture, yogurt, basil and salt and pepper until thoroughly mixed. Adjust the seasoning before serving. Serve with fresh salad leaves, pasta or egg salad or smoked fish such as smoked mackerel.

Makes 500 ml (18 fl oz/2¼ cups/33 tbsp).

Calories per tablespoon: 8 Kcals/34 Kj
Fat per tablespoon: 0.3 g

—MINT & YOGURT DRESSING—

1 clove garlic
300 ml (10 fl oz/1¼ cups) low fat plain yogurt
6 teaspoons semi-skimmed milk
2 tablespoons chopped fresh mint
salt and pepper

Peel and crush garlic. Put garlic, yogurt, milk, mint and salt and pepper in a bowl.

Whisk the ingredients together until thoroughly mixed. Cover and leave the dressing in a cool place for 30 minutes before serving, to allow the flavours to develop. Adjust the seasoning before serving.

Serve with a mixed bean salad or chicken salad.

Makes 350 ml (12 fl oz/1½ cups/23 tbsp).

Calories per tablespoon: 8 Kcals/34 Kj
Fat per tablespoon: 0.1 g

Variation: In place of the garlic and mint, add the finely grated rind and juice of 1 lemon or 1 lime.

ORANGE CINNAMON DRESSING

150 ml (5 fl oz/²⁄₃ cup) unsweetened orange juice
6 tablespoons white wine vinegar
12 teaspoons sunflower oil
finely grated rind and juice of 1 orange
1 teaspoon ground cinnamon
salt and pepper

Put orange juice, vinegar, oil, orange rind and squeezed juice, cinnamon and salt and pepper in a bowl and whisk the ingredients together until thoroughly mixed.

Alternatively, place all the ingredients in a clean jam jar. Screw top on jar and shake until all the ingredients are thoroughly mixed.

Adjust the seasoning before serving. Serve with fresh salad leaves, pasta salad, cooked or raw vegetables or cold sliced pork.

Makes 300 ml (10 fl oz/1¼ cups/20 tbsp).

Calories per tablespoon: 30 Kcals/123 Kj
Fat per tablespoon: 3 g

Variation: Use all freshly squeezed orange juice for extra flavour.

APPLE YOGURT DRESSING

450 g (1 lb) eating apples
300 ml (10 fl oz/1¼ cups) low fat plain yogurt
25 g (1 oz) preserved stem ginger
6 teaspoons syrup from stem ginger
6 teaspoons sweet sherry or apple liqueur
white pepper, to taste

Peel, core and slice apples thinly. Put apples in a saucepan with 3 tablespoons water, cover and cook until apples are soft, stirring occasionally.

Remove pan from heat and mash apples thoroughly with a fork or potato masher. Set aside to cool. In a bowl, whisk together the cooled apple purée and yogurt.

Chop the stem ginger finely and whisk into the yogurt mixture with the ginger syrup, sherry or apple liqueur and white pepper to taste. Mix the ingredients together well and adjust the seasoning before serving. Serve with a crisp fresh salad or sliced meats such as ham or pork.

Makes 675 ml (24 fl oz/3 cups/45 tbsp).

Calories per tablespoon: 10 Kcals/41 Kj
Fat per tablespoon: 0.07 g

—GARLIC & GINGER DRESSING—

2 cloves garlic
2.5 cm (1 in) piece fresh root ginger
7 tablespoons cider vinegar
6 teaspoons light soy sauce
3 teaspoons sunflower oil
3 teaspoons sesame oil
salt and pepper

Peel and crush garlic cloves. Peel and chop or grate ginger finely.

Put garlic, ginger, vinegar, soy sauce, sun-flower oil, sesame oil and salt and pepper a bowl. Whisk ingredients together until thoroughly mixed. Alternatively, put all the ingredients in a clean jam jar. Screw top on jar and shake until all the ingredients are thoroughly mixed.

Adjust the seasoning before serving. Serve with a fresh mixed salad, root vegetables, a mixed bean salad or grilled chicken or turkey.

Makes 175 ml (6 fl oz/¾ cup/11 tbsp).

Calories per tablespoon: 28 Kcals/114 Kj
Fat per tablespoon: 2.7 g

– CORIANDER & LIME DRESSING –

150 ml (5 fl oz/²⁄₃ cup) white grape juice
6 tablespoons white wine vinegar
12 teaspoons sunflower oil
2 tablespoons chopped fresh coriander
finely grated rind of 1 lime
juice of 2 limes
1 teaspoon caster sugar
salt and pepper

Put grape juice, vinegar, oil, coriander, lime rind, lime juice, sugar and salt and pepper in a bowl.

Whisk ingredients together until thoroughly mixed. Alternatively, put all the ingredients in a clean jam jar. Screw top on jar and shake until all the ingredients are thoroughly mixed.

Adjust the seasoning before serving. Serve with fresh salad leaves, fish or cold sliced meats.

Makes 350 ml (12 fl oz/1½ cups/23 tbsp).

Calories per tablespoon: 28 Kcals/114 Kj
Fat per tablespoon: 2.6 g

Variation: In place of the lime rind and juice, use lemon or orange rind and a mixture of chopped fresh herbs, such as parsley, thyme and basil.

— BANANA YOGURT DRESSING —

2 bananas
300 ml (10 fl oz/1¼ cups) low fat plain yogurt
9 teaspoons clear honey
¼ teaspoon ground mixed spice

Peel and slice bananas and put them in a bowl. Mash bananas thoroughly with a fork or potato masher.

Add yogurt, honey and mixed spice and stir the ingredients together until well mixed. Cover and leave the sauce in a cool place for 30 minutes before serving, to allow the flavours to develop.

Serve with fresh salad leaves, pasta salad or a mixed fruit and vegetable salad.

Makes 525 ml (19 fl oz/2⅓ cups/35 tbsp).

Calories per tablespoon: 14 Kcals/59 Kj
Fat per tablespoon: 0.09 g

Variation: In place of the mixed spice, add ¼ teaspoon ground ginger to the dressing.

——RASPBERRY VINAIGRETTE——

400 g (14 oz) can raspberries in fruit juice
8 tablespoons red wine vinegar
5 tablespoons sunflower oil
1 teaspoon caster sugar
1 teaspoon dried sage
salt and pepper

Put raspberries and juice in a blender or food processor and blend until smooth.

Strain raspberry purée through a nylon sieve and discard pips. Put raspberry juice, vinegar, oil, sugar, sage and salt and pepper in a bowl. Whisk the ingredients together until thoroughly mixed.

Alternatively, put all the ingredients in a clean jam jar. Screw top on jar and shake until ingredients are thoroughly mixed. Adjust the seasoning before serving. Serve with fresh salad leaves, rice salad, avocado or cold sliced meats such as chicken.

Makes 500 ml (18 fl oz/2¼ cups/33 tbsp).

Calories per tablespoon: 30 Kcals/123 Kj
Fat per tablespoon: 2.3 g

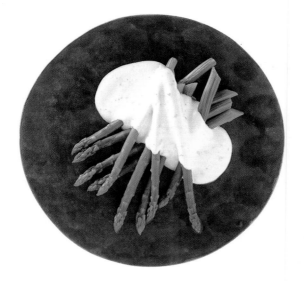

—FRESH TARRAGON DRESSING—

175 g (6 oz) low fat soft cheese
150 ml (5 fl oz/⅔ cup) reduced fat single (light) cream
  or low fat yogurt
2 tablespoons chopped fresh tarragon
1 tablespoon tarragon vinegar
salt and pepper

Put soft cheese and cream in a bowl and mix well.

Stir in tarragon, vinegar and salt and pepper, mixing well. Cover and leave the dressing in a cool place for 30 minutes before serving, to allow the flavours to develop. Adjust the seasoning before serving.

Serve with asparagus or hot or cold sliced meats such as chicken or turkey.

Makes 325 ml (11 fl oz/1⅓ cups/21 tbsp).

Calories per tablespoon: 24 Kcals/99 Kj
Fat per tablespoon: 1.9 g

Variation: Use semi-skimmed milk in place of the cream or yogurt, for an even lower calorie/lower fat dressing.

Calories per tablespoon: 18 Kcals/75 Kj
Fat per tablespoon: 1.3 g

INDEX